The
Heart of England
Way

Roger Noyce

Published by Sigma Leisure – an imprint of
Sigma Press, 1 South Oak Lane, Wilmslow, Cheshire SK9 6AR, England.

British Library Cataloguing in Publication Data
A CIP record for this book is available from the British Library.

ISBN: 1-85058-694-2

Typesetting and Design by: Sigma Press, Wilmslow, Cheshire.

Cover design: The Agency, Macclesfield – *The Heart of England Way logo is reproduced by permission.*
Photography: Roger and Margaret Noyce
Maps: The Author

Printed by: MFP Design and Print

Disclaimer: the information in this book is given in good faith and is believed to be correct at the time of publication. No responsibility is accepted by either the author or publisher for errors or omissions, or for any loss or injury howsoever caused. Only you can judge your own fitness, competence and experience.

Foreword

by **John Watts**,

co-founder of The Heart of England Way and
Information Officer for The Heart of England Way
Association

The Heart of England Way started life back in the 1970s when several
local rambling clubs joined forces to map out a 100-mile route from the
Cotswolds to Cannock Chase. Although it has generous support from
the Countryside Commission and other local bodies today, the prime
responsibility for the maintenance and promotion of the route still lies
firmly in the hands of committed local volunteers at the Heart of England Way Association.

For this reason I warmly welcome the publication of this new guide-
book, which I hope brings many new walkers to the footpaths of 'The
Way'. I am particularly pleased that it brings attention to a point that
The Association works hard to promote – the route is not just for the
long-distance enthusiast! Roger Noyce's thoughtful route plans, which
use sections of the full 100 miles, open up many opportunities for circular half, or full day walks. Now, using this new book, more people of all
ability levels will be encouraged to try out this inspirational route.

So – enthusiasts and day walkers alike – welcome to The Heart of
England! This route, which has been a part of my life for the past 30
years, links the lush hilly countryside of three Heart of England counties, and provides an excellent introduction to the area. I hope that you
enjoy your walks, whether you use Roger Noyce's book to tackle the
whole walking way, or simply spend an afternoon trying out one of his
excellent circular routes.

John Watts

Preface

The sun rising over rolling hills, the peace and quiet of a picturesque English village, the sparkle of a country river meandering through a scenic valley, the distinctive carpet of bluebells in a peaceful woodland, reflections on canals and lakes on a bright summer's day and the solitude of moors and heathland – these are a few of my favourite things that I can enjoy along the Heart of England Way. Although seemingly never far away from the hustle and bustle of the urban life of the cities of Birmingham and Coventry, the Heart of England Way carves a delightful route through the attractive countryside of the Midlands between Milford on Cannock Chase and Bourton-on-the-Water in the Cotswolds.

The first intentions to establish a walking way through the Midlands originated with the Alcester Civic Society. It, with a group of rambling and local walking clubs, promoted the route as long ago as 1978 and formed the Heart of England Way Association. Due to their efforts and persistence an initial route was introduced connecting Lichfield with Chipping Campden. In 1979 this became an 84-mile route from Milford to Chipping Campden, forming a useful walking link between the Staffordshire and the Cotswold Ways. The persistence of the Association gained the support of parish councils, and in the late 1980s the Countryside Commission took an influential interest. Finally, in 1990 the Way was officially recognised as a Long-Distance Path. Gloucestershire, Warwickshire and Staffordshire County Councils and Solihull MBC recognise the Way as a Recreation Path.

In 1992, the route was further extended into the Cotswold Area of Outstanding Natural Beauty so that today it is a 100-mile Long-Distance Path from Milford to Bourton-on-the-Water, and now also links with the Oxfordshire, Warden and Windrush Ways. Apart from being a very fine recreational walk for local walkers, the Heart of England Way now offers a fine link for anyone who attempts to walk from Land's End to John O'Groats. It is also projected to be a part of the European E2 route from Dover to Stranraer, which is scheduled to come into effect around the millennium. The Heart of England Way Association has been the driving force through all of this development and I am grateful to them for their interest, support and encouragement in the production of this book.

I recommend that you spare time to visit some of the many places of interest on the route of or near to the Heart of England Way. There are many attractive local circular walks and I have included 20 of these in the book. They vary in length from 3½ to 7 miles, and each one is designed to permit you to explore the nearby beauty of the Midlands and to enjoy refreshment at a local pub of character.

Like any author of walking books, I have a great affection for the beautiful countryside where I have lived for much of my life:

> *'So often have I walked the Way*
> *through picture village while farmers make hay.*
> *There are cottages of thatch, old churches in tone*
> *and historic old buildings in a mixture of stone.*
>
> *So often have I walked at pace*
> *along the Cotswold hills to Cannock Chase.*
> *The towns by the Way buzz with life and seem near*
> *as do those pubs selling their local beer.*
>
> *So often have I walked the Season*
> *along this very fine Way, with pleasure my reason.*
> *In Spring, in Summer, Autumn and Winter too*
> *this route is a delight, so fresh and so new.'*

I invite you to walk the Heart of England Way. I am sure that you too will come to appreciate its varied appeal.

Roger Noyce

Contents

Planning

The Heart of England Way: North to South

The Heart of England Way: South to North

20 Circular Walks

Planning

Experienced long-distance walkers know that there is no substitute for good planning if a walk is to be successful and enjoyable. Good forward planning will avoid many of the difficulties that can lead to a miserable walk, and the planning can, in fact, be part of the pleasure of the walk. Take time to explore the splendid scenery, potter about, visit local pubs, churches and sites of historical interest – simply enjoy the walk to the full. The whole area surrounding the Heart of England Way is a delight and there is little pleasure in plodding on at a fixed distance each day if you end up seeing very little.

The Heart of England Way can conveniently be walked in either direction (Bourton-on-the-Water to Milford or Milford to Bourton-on-the-Water), and this book provides a full description for whichever direction is selected. Whatever approach is adopted, it is important to build a plan of how you intend to complete the Way.

As a general guide, the Heart of England Way will take about nine days of walking to complete. It may be walked on a piecemeal basis, walking individual days over a period and perhaps travelling from home each day. Alternatively it can be walked over a couple of weeks with breaks to visit local places of interest, using bed and breakfast establishments or perhaps a caravan or tent for accommodation. Most day walkers are content to walk about 10 to 15 miles a day. Suggested 9-day itineraries are shown overleaf.

Equipment and Safety

The variety of countryside through which the Way passes is one of its main attractions. This changes from level walking along the banks of the Birmingham and Fazeley Canal to more strenuous sections over the Cotswold Hills. The author recommends the following as the basic equipment requirements when walking the Heart of England Way:

❀ walking boots

❀ warm and waterproof clothing

❀ a strong day rucksack

❀ food and liquid refreshment sufficient for the length of walk selected

❀ maps and the Heart of England Way book

❀ a compass

When walking the circular routes you should dress according to the length of the walk and the day's weather forecast.

The route of the Heart of England Way

From	To	Miles	Kilometres
Milford	Castle Ring	8¾	14
Castle Ring	Weeford	11¼	18
Weeford	Kingsbury	9¼	15
Kingsbury	Meriden	13½	22
Meriden	Rowington	11¼	18
Rowington	Alcester	12½	20
Alcester	Upper Quinton	11½	18
Upper Quinton	Blockley	10	16
Blockley	Bourton-on-the-Water	12	19
Total Distance		*100*	*160*

North to South

From	To	Miles	Kilometres
Bourton-on-the-Water	Blockley	12	19
Blockley	Upper Quinton	10	16
Upper Quinton	Alcester	11½	18
Alcester	Rowington	12½	20
Rowington	Meriden	11¼	18
Meriden	Kingsbury	13½	22
Kingsbury	Weeford	9¼	15
Weeford	Castle Ring	11¼	18
Castle Ring	Milford	8¾	14
Total Distance		*100*	*160*

South to North

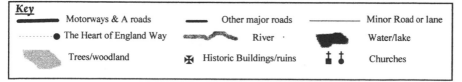

Key

━━━ Motorways & A roads	━━ Other major roads	—— Minor Road or lane
⋯⋯● The Heart of England Way	River ·	Water/lake
Trees/woodland	✠ Historic Buildings/ruins	Churches

Key to symbols used on maps

Maps

The maps in this book are at an approximate scale of 1:32,500 and should prove adequate for a successful completion of the Heart of England Way. The scale of the maps for the circular walks varies. *The key to the map symbols is on the preceding page.*

It is prudent for the walker to acquire Ordnance Survey maps. The entire route is covered by Landranger maps (scale 1:50,000) and a mixture of Outdoor Leisure, Pathfinder and Explorer maps (scale 1:25,000). For planning the route and travelling, 1:50,000 maps provide a very broad perspective while the 1:25,000 maps are most helpful for the walk itself. The following maps cover the route, but do look for the new Explorer maps that will be issued during 1999.

Landranger series

- ❀ 163 – Cheltenham and Cirencester, Stow-on-the-Wold
- ❀ 151 – Stratford-upon-Avon, Warwick and Banbury
- ❀ 150 – Worcester and the Malverns
- ❀ 140 – Leicester, Coventry and Rugby
- ❀ 139 – Birmingham
- ❀ 128 – Derby and Burton upon Trent
- ❀ 127 – Stafford and Telford, Ironbridge

Pathfinder series

- ❀ 1020 – Vale of Evesham
- ❀ 997 – Stratford-upon-Avon (West) and Alcester
- ❀ 975 – Redditch and Henley-in-Arden
- ❀ 955 – Coventry (South) and Kenilworth
- ❀ 935 – Coventry (North) and Meriden
- ❀ 914 – Nuneaton
- ❀ 913 – Sutton Coldfield and Walsall
- ❀ 892 – Lichfield and Brownhills

Outdoor Leisure/Explorer

Outdoor Leisure 45 – The Cotswolds Explorer 6 – Cannock Chase and Chasewater. Explorer 6 replaces Pathfinders 850 Stafford, 871 Cannock North, and 872 Rugeley and Lichfield [North].

Places of Interest

There are many historic and other places of interest to visit on and around the Heart of England Way and this book provides general information to assist you. Wherever a place name appears in bold within the walks, you will find a detailed description of the place in the final section of this book. The information is listed by place name in alphabetical order.

Dogs

Dogs must be kept on leads at all times. If you are walking the Way during lambing time, in April and May, and/or when calves are in the fields with the cows, it is better to leave your dog at home.

Information

Information on the Heart of England Way is available from The Heart of England Way Association, 20

Throckmorton Road, Alcester B49 6QA. Send a SAE for a free up-to-date list of hotels and B&Bs. They also sell rucksack badges (£1.20) and certificates (£1.00).

Tourist information is available from information centres and libraries along the Way. The following are happy to provide more detailed information and have a variety of books on the Way:

Lichfield Tourist Information. Telephone 01543 252109

County Library, Henley-in-Arden. Telephone 01564 792965

Warwick Information Centre. Telephone 01926 492212

Alcester Library. Telephone 01789 762430

Evesham Information Centre. Telephone 01386 446944

Stratford-upon-Avon Information Centre. Telephone 01789 293127

Chipping Campden Information Centre. Telephone 01386 840101

Stow-on-the-Wold Information Centre. Telephone 01451 831082

Car Parking

For those using cars for transport while walking the Heart of England Way, the following is a list of possible parking places, complete with grid references:

Bourton-on-the-Water: Station Road Pay & Display Car Park has toilets. SP 169204

Blockley: The small free village centre car park has toilets. SP 164350

Upper Quinton: Park on the wide grass verge in Tailor Road, near to the village green. SP 174465

Bidford-on-Avon: Free public car park by the road island in Bidford. SP 099519

Alcester: Park in the free car park (with toilets) in Moorfield Road at the rear of the High Street. SP 088575

Henley: Prince Harry Road car park (not Wednesday) SP 151657 or park by the roadside in Beaudesert Lane, Henley-in-Arden, SP 153659.

Rowington: Park with consideration in Mill Lane, SP 202694, or with permission in the church car park, SP 203692.

Meriden: Park in the road outside the Queen's Head Pub. SP 252821

Kingsbury: Park in the free car park in Peartree Avenue. SP 218963

Weeford: Park at side of track near to Jerry's Lane. SK 151058

Lichfield: Pay & Display car park in Pool Walk near to Minster Pool. SK 116097

Castle Ring: Park in free car park provided. SK 045125

Milford: Park in the free car park near to the Tourist Office. SJ 973211

Public Transport

For details approach the Travel Information Service of the appropriate local authority:

Staffordshire County Council. Telephone 01785 223344

Warwickshire County Council. Telephone 01926 410410

West Midlands (Centro). Telephone 0121 200 2700

Gloucestershire County Council Telephone 01452 425543

The Heart of England Way Association

Responsibility for the continued existence and development of the Way rests with the Heart of England Way Association, which receives support and encouragement from the official bodies but acts on a voluntary basis. The Association interacts with the official representatives, who form a liaison committee that meets annually under the auspices of Warwickshire County Council. It is concerned with general development issues, resolution of any major problems arising, and the reporting of progress.

Apart from its official duties in the wardenship and maintenance of the Heart of England Way, the Association holds regular guided walks along and around the Way and its members receive newsletters and a guided walks programme.

For information on membership of the Heart of England Way Association, contact The Heart of England Way Association, 20 Throckmorton Road, Alcester B49 6QA.

Waymarking

The whole route is clearly waymarked throughout with Heart of England Way symbols, tall finger-posts or metal road signs. The symbol is the name of the Way on a dark green oak leaf. This may be a separate symbol or may be set in the centre of the normal yellow (footpaths) and blue (bridleway) waymarkers used by the various local authorities. The circular walks have waymarks in the normal yellow or blue form.

Access and the Country Code

The Heart of England Way is set along proven rights of way and permissive routes comprising paths, bridleways and public roads. The Way passes through a most beautiful part of the country and walkers are requested to treasure the access facility granted and to always keep to the footpath when walking the Heart of England Way. Avoid taking short cuts or walking parallel paths and always follow the Country Code wherever you walk.

❀ Fasten all gates

❀ Keep dogs under proper control

❀ Avoid damaging fences, hedges and walls

❀ Keep to paths across farmland

❀ Leave no litter

❀ Safeguard water supplies

❀ Protect wildlife, wild plants and trees

❀ Walk carefully on country roads

❀ Respect the life of the countryside

The Heart of England Way: North to South

Malt Mill Lane, Alcester

Milford to Castle Ring

Distance: 8¾ miles (14km)

Duration: 5 hours

Terrain: Easy walking over heathland and through delightful woodland on Cannock Chase.

Place names: throughout the route descriptions, wherever a place name appears in bold within the walks, you will find a detailed description of the place in the final section of this book.

From the free car park by the Tourist Office on **Milford Common** (with **Shugborough Hall** across the A512), go initially north-east towards the A512 then, in about 70 metres, go right, ascending onto **Cannock Chase**. Now follow the clear path south past two small lakes. In about 500 metres, bear left (south-east) on a green track which leads past Mere Pits (ponds on your right). It then arcs right (south-west) up Mere Valley be-

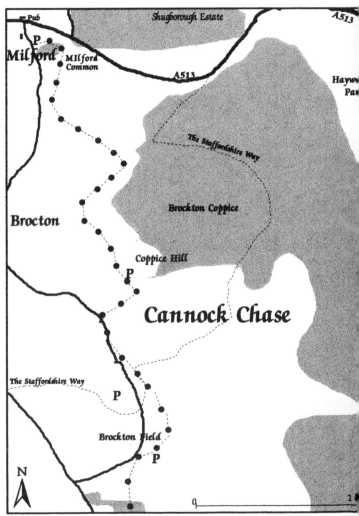

fore veering left (south-east), taking you onto the moorland of the Chase.

This delightful stretch of walking continues with fine views all around as you meander the clear track past the car park on Coppice Hill. Soon you will cross over the Staffordshire Way near Glacial Boulder. Continue by arcing to reach the car park at Chase Road corner, then go over Anson's Bank to arrive on a road. Go left along the roadside for 50 metres then go left again on a stone track. Pass by the Katyn Memorial to some 14,000 Polish soldiers who gave their lives in their Second World Wat, and continue west into woodlands. The track soon veers right to progress south-east through the fine Cannock Chase woodland then to cross a road and reach a second road at Flints Corner.

Cross over the road and continue south-east along Marquis Drive. In about 200 metres bear left on a tarmac lane (with a Visitor Centre to your right) and soon you will onter woodland once again. The route line becomes east. The fine walking on a forest track leads down to a railway line. Cross

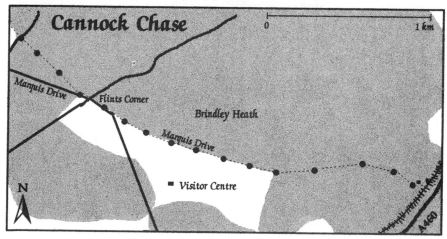

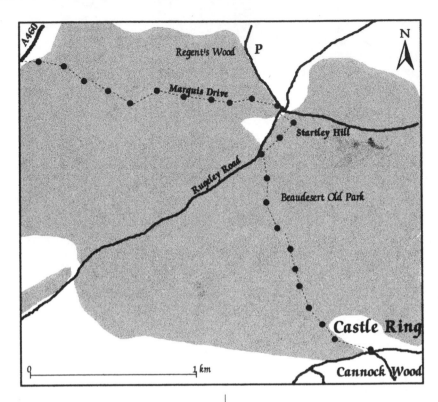

then proceed with care over the fast A460. Continue along Marquis Drive by ascending the narrow lane opposite with a stream on your left. Pass by Seven Springs and some forestry cottages and you will soon arrive at a road junction. Cross over the road at the junction and proceed on a path to the right and opposite. The path soon

veers right to progress near to the Rugeley Road for some 300 metres. It then bends left (almost south), becoming a wide green track as it descends through the trees of Beaudesert Old Park. The track passes a pond then climbs for about 700 metres, when you bear left into the trees to arrive at **Castle Ring**.

Castle Ring to Weeford

Distance: 11¼ miles (18km)

Duration: 6 hours

Terrain: Easy walking. Initially over moorland on the edge of Cannock Chase and then over pleasant countryside leading to the magnificent Lichfield Cathedral. The final part comprises a fine track walk to reach Packington Moor.

From the car park at **Castle Ring**, walk out to Holly Hill Road and go left past a pub. There are houses to the right and Broad Hazels woodland across a field to the left. Where the road goes sharp right, proceed ahead through a kissing gate and walk a fenced path with a reservoir to your right. In 150 metres go right and continue through a second kissing gate at a road junction in Gentleshaw. Go ahead, passing a school and then a brick-built church on your left.

About 80 metres beyond the church bear right on to Gentleshaw Common on a clear path going in a south-east direction. The path (known as Common Side) continues with the road and some attractive houses to its left for about three-quarters of a mile (1.4km), until you reach a junction of roads.

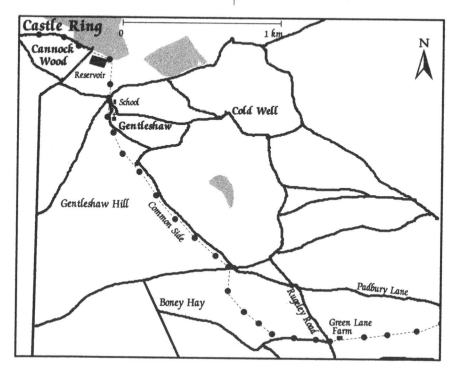

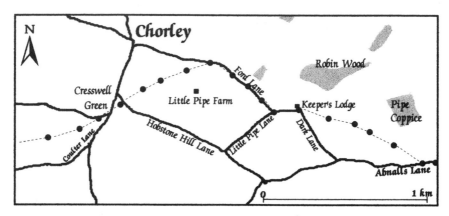

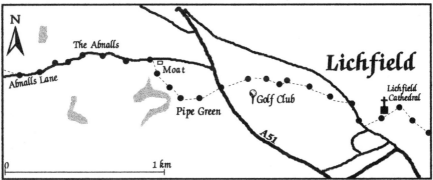

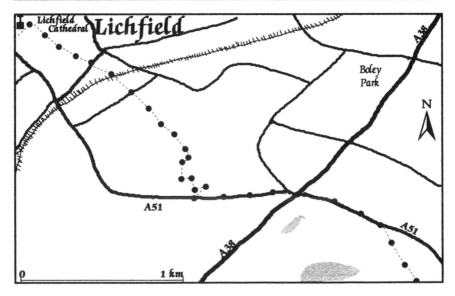

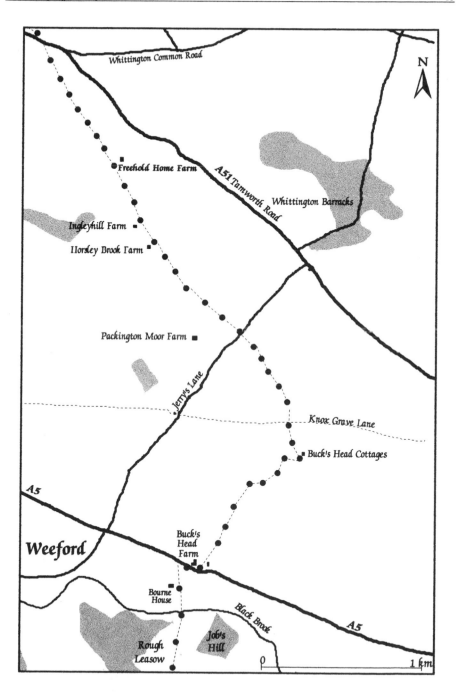

Whittington Common Road

N

Freehold Home Farm

A51 Tamworth Road

Whittington Barracks

Ingleyhill Farm

Horsley Brook Farm

Packington Moor Farm

Jerry's Lane

Knox Grave Lane

Buck's Head Cottages

A5

Weeford

Buck's Head Farm

Bourne House

Black Brook

A5

Rough Leasow

Job's Hill

0   1 km

Cross over the road and go over a stile set to the right of Padbury Lane. Descend south over pastureland to go over a stile and footbridge over Redmoor Brook. Now bear left to walk the path as it follows the brook, which meanders south-west. At the field end, go over a stile and go left to walk a lane past a pub. Walk the lane/track in a generally easterly direction; going over Rugeley Road and reaching Padbury Lane, which leads into Creswell Green. Continue ahead, going over a footbridge and on to Hobstone Hill Lane.

Cross the lane and go over the stile opposite. Follow a path by the side of Bilston Brook as it proceeds over fields and stiles to reach Ford Lane. Go right and walk Ford Lane until you reach a keeper's lodge on the lane corner. Immediately after passing the lodge, go left over a stile and proceed on the clear path descending east over cultivated fields and stiles. There are pleasant views all around. You will cross Ashmore Brook before climbing to reach Abnalls Lane via a stile. Go left along the lane for the next 900 metres, passing by The Abnalls, with attractive rock formations lining the road.

Just past the entrance to Maple Hayes Hall (a dyslexia school), go right and walk a hedged track passing an ancient moat on your left. Go over a stile and then a footbridge with The Dell on your right. A delightful stretch of walking on to Pipe Green proceeds over fields and stiles as it veers left (north-east) to reach the A515.

Cross the A515 and go over the stile opposite with a golf course to your right. Follow the clear waymarkers as you navigate around the top of the golf course and football pitches and walk the back of a row of houses. You pass a recreation area to arrive in Shaw Lane, **Lichfield**.

Proceed up Shaw Lane to Bird Street, where you go right then left into The Close for a magnificent view of Lichfield Cathedral. Walk past the Cathedral and bear right down Dam Street, ever alert for some fine brass waymarkers set in the pavements of the city. Proceed ahead through the main shopping area and go through the arcade to reach the A5127. Cross the road at the pedestrian crossing and walk up to Station Road.

Bear left and then when you reach the Philadelphian Hall, go right over the railway line and walk a series of footpaths crossing over Cherry Orchard and into Oakhurst Road. Bear off right to continue over Manor Rise and to arrive in a cul-de-sac called Hillside by a lamp-post. Go right and descend into Quarry Hills Lane. Go sharp right to reach the A51 Tamworth road. Now go left and walk the pavement of the A51 for 650 metres, going over the A38 road bridge.

In a further 500 metres, cross over the A51 to progress up a green lane and to go through a gate onto a track which continues in a south-east line for just over 1½ miles (2.6km), until you arrive at the parking area by Jerry's Lane. You will go over a series of fields, gates and stiles and pass by Freeford Home, Ingleyhill and Horsley Brook Farms, and Packington Moor Farm will be to your right as you arrive at Jerry's Lane.

Weeford to Kingsbury

Distance: 9¼ miles (15km)

Duration: 5½ hours

Terrain: An easy walk in typical Warwickshire countryside. Rough Leasows is particularly attractive and there is a pleasing towpath walk leading to the delightful Kingsbury Water Park

From the track-side park area, walk south-east to cross over Jerry's Lane and continue on the clear track for three-quarters of a mile (1.2km), going through a gate by Knox's Grave lane and eventually reaching Buck's Head Cottages. Here, go right (west) for some 130 metres then go left to descend fields in a generally south-south-west direction, passing between the buildings of Buck's Head Farm to reach the busy A5.

Cross over the A5 with care and go right for some 90 metres, then go left down a lane to cross over a bridge over Black Brook. Go over a stile to walk a path going south. This delightful stretch of walking (three-quarters of a mile) passes between two woodland plantations,

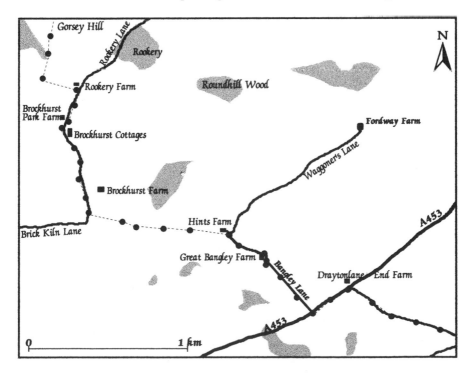

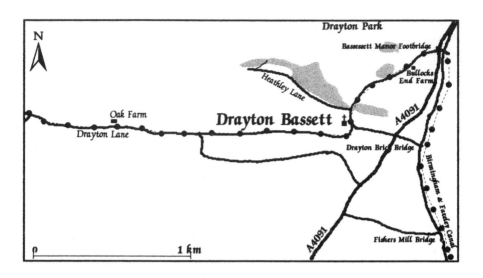

goes over a couple of stiles then climbs the beautiful valley of Rough Leasow to reach woodland near to Gorsley Hill. Go over the stile near the top and descend to the left of a hedge to go over a further stile onto a farm track. Now go left along the track, passing between the converted buildings of Rookery Farm to reach Rookery Lane.

Go right and walk Rookery Lane for just over half a mile, passing by Brockhurst Farm. One hundred metres beyond the farm go left and up a field, going generally south-east to reach a hedge stile. Go over the stile and descend over fields to arrive on a lane by Hints Farm via a gate. Walk past the farm, bearing right to Bangley Lane. After passing Great Bangley Farm you will soon reach the A453, where you go left. In 300 metres go right to walk Drayton Lane into the village of **Drayton Bassett**. At the road T-junction go left to walk through the village, passing the church, the post office and Bullock's End Farm to arrive at the A4091.

Cross the road, bearing slightly left to go over an ornate, white, castellated bridge over the **Birmingham and Fazeley Canal**. Now go right and walk the towpath of the canal for about 2½ miles (3.5km). Pass beneath Fisher's Mill bridge and later a swivel bridge to arrive by a camping and caravan site. Follow the Heart of England Waymarkers as the path zigzags to become a lane, passing by Moorash Farm. It then veers sharp left and becomes a walking track as it proceeds beneath the M42 to enter **Kingsbury Water Park**.

Continue on the waymarked path towards the park as it arcs to the right to a junction of paths with lakes ahead. (After going beneath the M42 road bridge you could have detoured to go to the Park's Visitor Centre by going right. From the Centre, go east along the lakeside path.)

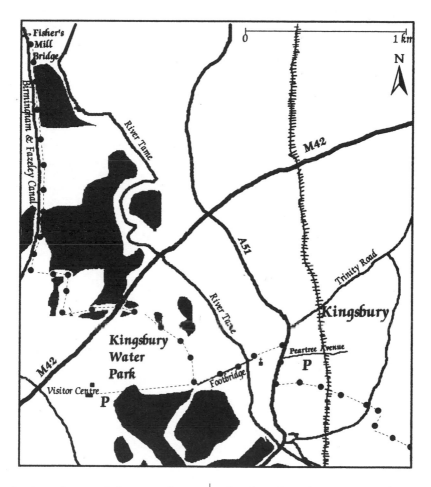

At the junction, go left over a long, wooden, raised footbridge and continue over the footbridge over the River Tame. Proceed up the steps to arrive by the side of the churchyard then bear slightly left by the side of the churchyard to arrive at the road in the town of Kingsbury. Bear right to reach the A51 then right again for about 100 metres before crossing the A51 to enter Pear Tree Avenue. There is a car park on the right.

Kingsbury to Meriden

Distance: 13½ miles (22km)

Duration: 7½ hours

Terrain: Easy walking. The reservoir at Shustoke is worthy of exploration; the bluebells in Dumble Woods are a picture in spring and the walk through Meriden Shafts is a true pleasure.

From the car park in Pear Tree Avenue in Kingsbury, retrace your steps to the A51 and go left along its pavement for 200 metres. Next go left through a small grassland area, bearing right to walk a path at the back (left) of residential gardens. In 300 metres, cross over the main railway line and go over a stile to walk the clear path in a south-east direction and to cross over a lane with a rifle range ahead.

Bear right and circle the perimeter of the range. Go left at its end before veering off to the right, initially going north-east and then turning towards Camp Farm. Walk the farm drive to a road near the village of Hurley. Go left along the road for 100 metres then go right into a lane, proceeding over a stile onto a clear path going south. Walk this path for some 500 metres then bear left to reach Dexter's Lane.

Go right along Dexter's Lane and continue until you reach a lane junction at Foul End. Proceed ahead on to a track that soon becomes a path as it arcs south-west over wide open fields. In about three-quarters of a mile (1.2km) you will go through a gate into a small copse where Highland cattle may be running free. Proceed through the copse and through a small woodland to reach and cross

the B4098. Go over a stile to enter and to descend the field opposite, going south-west over three further stiles to reach a road near Whitacre Heath.

Go right for about 100 metres then cross the road to veer right down a lane past houses. Now go left along a clear path to the left of the railway. In about 500 metres you will go over a footbridge. Arc left to a second footbridge and then a stone stile by a farm lane. Bear right to proceed south over the next field then go over a stile to diagonally cross the next field to a lane. Cross the lane, go over a stile and descend a hedge-side path to reach a stile on to the railway line.

On the other side of the railway line, go left and walk the line-side path for just over three-quarters of a mile (1.3km). Now go right through a hand gate and in about 150 metres you will reach a junction of paths. Go right to follow the Heart of England Waymarkers into cultivated land. At the field corner, go left then bear right to climb over stiles and to reach Church Road (near the village of Church End).

Cross the A4114 and proceed over the stile opposite to walk the edge of fields. At the corner of the third field go left, and then at the end of this field go right over a stile to

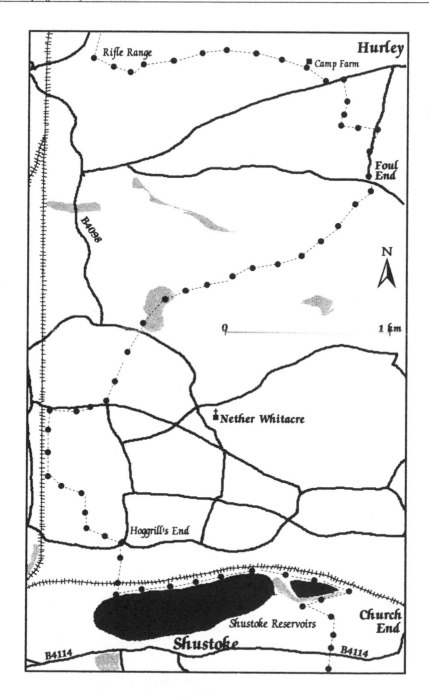

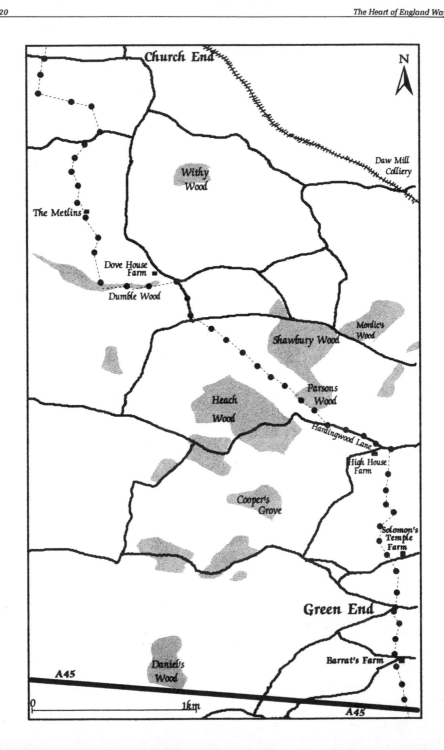

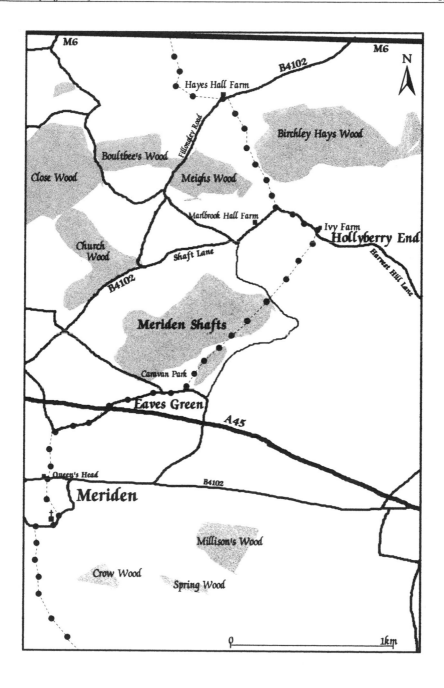

continue south. In about 250 metres you will go over a stile on to a lane. Go right to leave the lane at its next corner and continue south over fields for just over three-quarters of a mile (1.3km). You will go over several stiles and footbridges and pass by The Metlins before descending over a stile into Dumble Wood (which is full of bluebells in the spring). The path bears left above a small stream. The half-timbered Dove House Farm is an attractive picture across the stream. All too soon you will arrive at a lane where you go right until you reach a road junction.

Cross over the road, go over a tiny stream and commence an 850-metre walk over a very large field, aiming for a stile to the right of Parson's Wood. Continue along the wood edge then diagonally cross the next small field to go over a stile to Hardingwood Lane. Go left along the lane for 400 metres then go right over a stile to continue south over a series of fields and stiles. Just after passing Solomon's Temple Farm you will cross a lane and can proceed over a stile to reach the road in Green End. Continue south over a road junction then walk a path over pastureland for some 800 metres. You will go over a series of stiles, pass by Barratt's Farm and cross a footbridge over the M6.

Some 300 metres beyond the M6, bear left to reach a road next to Hayes Hall Farm. Go left along the road for about 75 metres then go right over a stile and on to a path which meanders the right edge of Birchley Hays Wood, but maintains its south-east direction line to go over a footbridge and then a stile to a lane. Go left along the lane for 300 metres to reach the edge of Hollyberry End. Just after passing Ivy House Farm (on the left), leave the lane by going right on a hedged track. In about 600 metres you will go over a stile into woodland at Meriden Shafts.

Initially you go left, walking a track along the edge of the wood. Next go right to walk through this very attractive woodland, proceeding in a south-east direction on a clear path. Exit the woodland via a stile and continue south-west over common ground by a horse jumping area. After going over a further two stiles you will reach Eaves Green Road. Go right past a caravan park, continuing ahead at a road junction to go beneath the noisy A45. In about 700 metres you will arrive at The Queen's Head in Meriden, near to the B4102.

Meriden to Rowington

Distance: 11¼ miles (18km)

Duration: 6 hours

Terrain: Easy. Berkswell and Baddesley Clinton are particularly beautiful.

From the Queen's Head in Meriden, go up the steps and over the B4102, proceeding south through kissing gates to pass Meriden Church and to reach a lane. Go right along the lane past the church, and in 150 metres go left into pastureland. Initially head in a southerly direction, then after the first stile veering left (south-east) to continue over a series of fields and stiles to reach Back Lane. Cross the lane and continue on a path, now aiming generally south-west over

five fields before veering east past Blind Hall Farm. Next zigzag to reach the Meriden road near to the beautiful village of Berkswell. Go left to walk along the road, then, in about 200 metres, cross the road and go right through a small gate. Go over a stile to reach a kissing gate that allows you to walk the perimeter of the village churchyard before arriving in **Berkswell** via a further gate.

Go right to walk in front of the magnificent porch of the fine

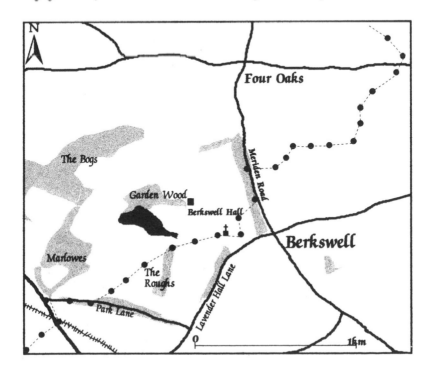

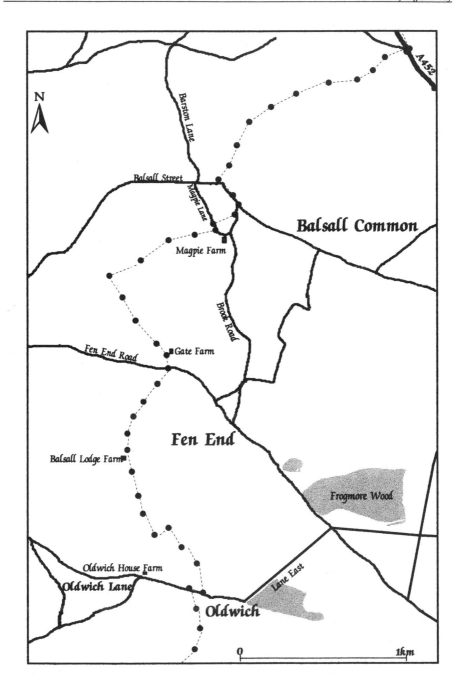

church, then continue through a kissing gate and stile to a long footbridge of planks. Berkswell Hall is to your right and a beautiful lake ahead to the right. Continue through trees, leaving via a kissing gate to walk The Roughs on a clear track going south-west. In about 650 metres you will reach a kissing gate to Park Lane. Go right to arrive at the busy A452. Cross over the A452 with great care and go left along the pavement for just over 200 metres. Now go right on a narrow lane passing near to Wootton Grange. Cross a footbridge to continue south-west over a series of fields and stiles and to reach Balsall Street via a final stile. Go left along the road for 200 metres then left again into Long Brook Lane.

After walking the lane for about 75 metres, the Way goes right over a stile to a further stile onto Magpie Lane. It then goes left for 60 metres to continue south-west across attractive cultivated fields before going over a footbridge and stiles to a junction of paths. (Alternatively, continue along the lane as it arcs right past the beautiful half-timbered Magpie Farm and in about 60 metres go left.) At the junction of paths, go left (south-east) to pass to the right of Gate Farm and onto Fen End Road. Cross the road and continue, now in a south-westerly direction, on a path which, after passing Balsall Lodge Farm, gently arcs left (south-east again) to go over a stile. Go left then in 90 metres go right over a stile to continue south-east over a series of fields and stiles to reach the hamlet of Oldwich.

Here, go right. In 80 metres go left over a stile to proceed over pleasing farm land, going over a number of stiles and footbridges. Some 450 metres after the second footbridge the path follows the fence to a stile. Here, aim north-west to diagonally cross the next field and to arrive at a stile into Priests Park Wood. Proceed through the attractive woodland, leaving it to go over a stile behind a row of houses. Now go left along the back of the houses then right through the housing estate to a lane that leads to the A4141 in Chadwick End.

Cross the A4141 then go left then right over a stile to continue in a south-south-west direction over a series of fields and stiles, passing an old convent building to arrive on Rising Lane. Now go right. At the next bend in Rising Lane continue ahead into Hay Wood Lane, passing by Manor Park Farm on the right. After walking the lane for about 300 metres, go right over stiles to pass Bromes Park. Go over a footbridge and through a bluebell copse to a gate to a lane that leads into **Baddesley Clinton**.

Walk to the left of the magnificent National Trust Manor Hall (nearby is **Packington Hall** another attractive National Trust property). Bear left along a path and via a kissing gate into Baddesley Clinton churchyard (it is a blaze of yellow daffodils in the spring). Go right through another gate and onto a path that leads over fields, going in a general south-west/south direction. The clear path arcs gently to the left as you go over a stile and passes through several gates to proceed to the left of Lyons Farm and to a lane.

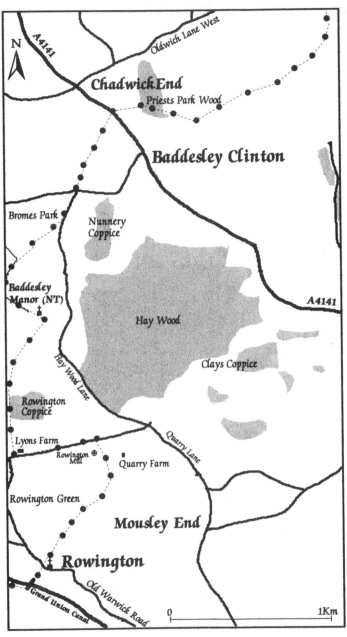

Go left along the lane for about 450 metres, passing by the superbly converted Rowington Mill. Go right through a gate into pastureland. The path starts in a south-west direction, passing Quarry Farm (to the left), then bends right to a stile to continue in a south-east direction. Go over three more fields and stiles to reach the churchyard at Rowington.

Rowington to Alcester

Distance: 12½ miles (20km)

Duration: 7 hours

Terrain: Mainly easy walking through rolling Warwickshire countryside.

From Rowington Church on the B4439 (old Warwick road), cross the road and descend the lane on the corner opposite to the church to reach the **Grand Union Canal**. Cross over the canal and go right to walk a path on the bank above the canal then bear left (south-west) to continue by hedges over several fields. In about 600 metres, go right (north-west), down a lane which runs parallel to the noisy M4 to emerge on Finwood Road.

Now go left to cross the M40 and to meander south-west down Finwood Road to reach the hamlet of Finwood, walking along the road as it becomes Mill Lane. You will cross over the Lapworth Canal at Finwood Bridge to reach Lapworth Street.

Cross Lapworth Street and walk the lane opposite through an attractive residential area. Soon the lane becomes a track. Go over a stile as you arrive in pastureland and zigzag right and then left to enter pleasant woodland. As you emerge from the trees you will see Coppice Farm on your right – a very pleasant stretch of walking takes you to a gate by the farm, where you go left onto a farm lane.

Walk this lane as it goes over a bridge over a dismantled railway. After 400 metres it reaches the Henley road via a gate. Go right around the bend in the road, and in 60 metres go right again into fields. Follow the clear waymarkers going generally south-west over a series of fields and

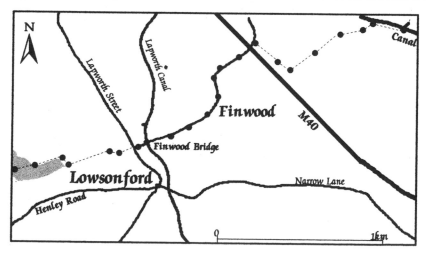

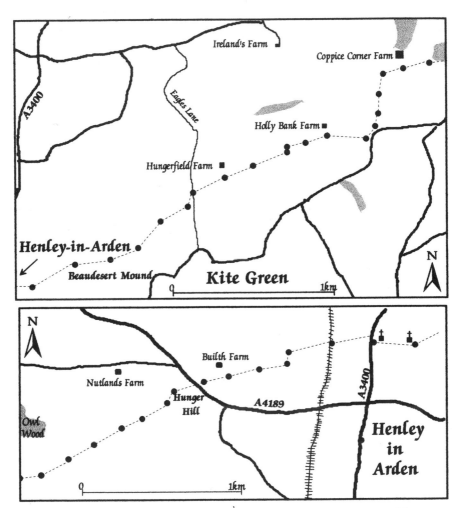

stiles. You will pass Hungerfield Farm (on your right) and cross over Edge Lane, then traverse the lovely hills of Beaudesert Mount before descending to go over a stile and on to a residential road near to the church in **Henley-in-Arden.**

Proceed up the road, going over a river bridge to arrive in the High Street (the A3400). Go right, cross the High Street via its pedestrian crossing then go left to enable you to go right through the old coaching entrance to the Swan Inn. Proceed past the picnic area behind the pub and climb a fenced/hedged path at the back of houses. In about 250 metres you will reach Station Road, where you go left then right to enter the Henley-in-Arden railway station complex.

Continue by going over the foot-

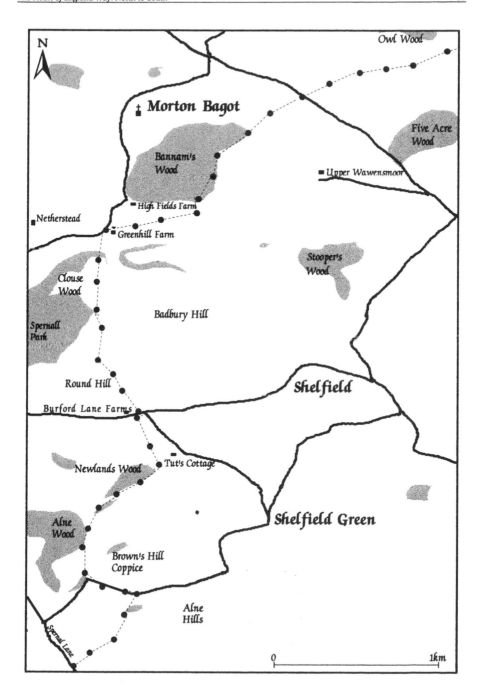

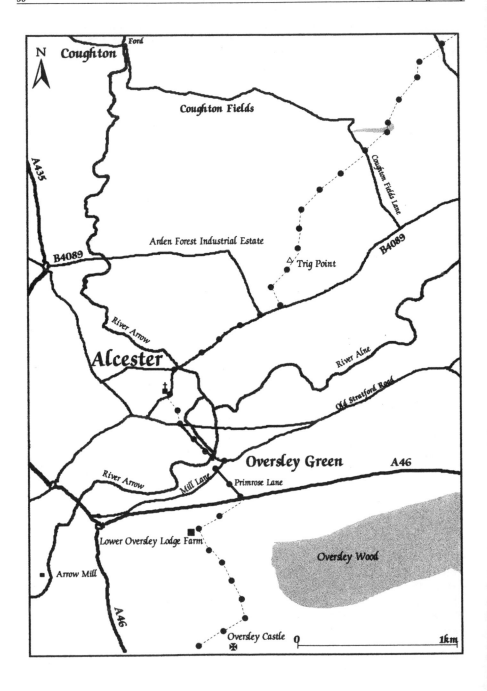

bridge over the railway lines and walk a fenced path at the back of allotments to reach a stile. Here, go left for 100 metres then right over a footbridge – you can now walk three fields in a south-westerly direction until you reach a stile to the A4189 at Hunger Hill. Cross the road and go over a superb brick stile set to the right of a house then continue through gates into a fenced area. The path leaves via a stile, aiming left (south) to a footbridge. Here bear slightly right on a clear path heading in a south-westerly direction. Keep this general direction for the next just over a mile (1.7km), going over a few stiles until you reach a lane.

Cross the lane and ascend the path opposite to the right of a hedge. Bannam's Wood is ahead. Walk the permissive footpath to the left of the wood and pause to enjoy the pleasing views at the hilltop. The path enters the trees over a stile and soon reaches the open and a hand gate. Now go right and walk to the left of a hedge, passing by a fishpond with High Fields Farm in the far right corner of the field. You will pass by the buildings of Greenhill Farm to arrive at a road via a gate. Go left along the road for 40 metres then go left again through a metal gate to descend south over a field and to go over a footbridge. Continue in a southerly direction through a copse and by a field hedge, going over a stile and then a large cultivated field to reach the

corner of Clouse Wood via a gateway. Here, bear left to a stile going generally south-south-east once again before walking a field hedge around the contour of Round Hill.

You will go over a couple of stiles to emerge on Burford Lane by a cottage. Go right along the lane for about 75 metres, then go left over a stile going south-south-east to reach a track. Walk the track for 60 metres then veer right over a stile to continue to the left of Newlands Wood. Continue

Pub sign for "Tom o' the Wood" near Rowington

to the right of trees near Lodge Hill before arcing left on to a farm track to the left of Alne Wood.

Walk this farm track as it continues to arc left to reach a lane at its corner. Go left along the lane for 400 metres then go right over a stile to a farm track. This leads to a farm lane and then a T-junction with Spernall Lane. Cross Spernall Lane, bearing left to go right over a stile by New End Cottages. Continue over a footbridge and further stiles as you walk generally south-west by the field hedge, always following the clear waymarkers. In about 500 metres you will cross over a farm track with a pond on the other side of the stile opposite. Now descend right, going over a stile to the right of the Canada Barn building to reach Coughton Fields Lane. Here, go left then in 25 metres go right through a farm gate to walk a wide farm track by the field hedge. The track becomes a path as it progresses over a stile and then goes left over a further stile before bearing right over the bridge of a dismantled railway.

After going over the bridge you will go over a couple of further stiles to a path which crosses a large cultivated field and pass a trig point (an impressive 66 metres!). From here there is a view of the town of Alcester. Go over the stile at the field end and descend through

trees to reach the B4089 in **Alcester**. Now go right and walk the pavement into the town centre.

Pass the Greig Memorial Hall on the right before crossing over a bridge over the River Arrow. Walk up Henley Street, passing to the right of the church to reach the High Street in this very attractive town. The main car park is behind the shops to the right of the High Street.

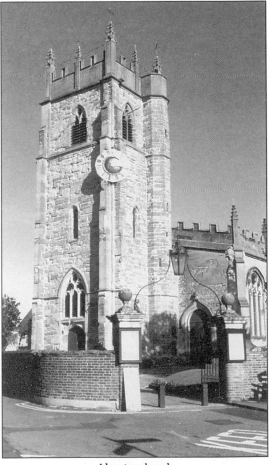

Alcester church

Alcester to Upper Quinton

Distance: 11½ miles (18km)

Duration: 6½ hours

Terrain: Mainly easy walking through pleasant countryside, plus some fine riverside walking.

From the car park in **Alcester**, enter the High Street via the shopping passageway and go left to walk past the church. At the left bend in the road, go right to stroll down the attractive Malt Mill Lane and to reach the River Arrow. Now go left and walk through the small, pleasant riverside park to reach and cross the old Stratford Road. Proceed by walking the lane opposite, which leads over a bridge where the Alne and the Arrow rivers meet to reach the village of Oversley Green.

At the road junction, go right into Mill Lane. In 125 metres go left again by beautiful thatched cottages to walk Primrose Lane and to cross over a footbridge over the busy A46. Go over the stile at the bridge end and go right up a farm lane towards Lower Oversley Lodge Farm, with its huge grain silos. Bear left past the silos and continue along the farm lane. You will have a good view of Ragley Hall to your right, with the white, castellated Oversley Castle ahead.

Follow the lane as it arcs to your right and then contours below the castle to reach its entrance road. The castle is privately owned so continue down the lane through pleasing countryside to reach a crossroads. The delightful Oversley Church is almost opposite. At the crossroads go right then immediately left to walk a

path to the left of the church. In 250 metres go left again to go over a stile into a small caravan park, which you will exit via a gate into the car park of the Fish Inn in Wixford.

Continue ahead, cross the road and walk the Way path through trees, with the River Arrow to your right as you go over footbridges. The Way veers to continue in a generally southerly direction over a series of fields, passing to the left of Moor Hall Farm complex and over stiles. It soon arrives in the village of Broom to emerge at a road near the Broom Tavern Inn. Cross the road and proceed along a hedged path opposite going between houses. It passes through a village playing field area and then arcs left over a field to go under a former railway bridge.

On the other side of the road, go right for 220 metres then bear left at a residential estate to enter a fenced path between houses. This proceeds at the back of a row of houses to arrive in a residential lane on the outskirts of the town of **Bidford on Avon**. Walk the lane as it bends left. In about 125 metres go right down a hedged lane between houses to cross the busy B439 and to arrive at the High Street in the town, emerging near to the Frog and Bulrush pub. Go left along the pavement then right over Bidford Bridge. Admire a de-

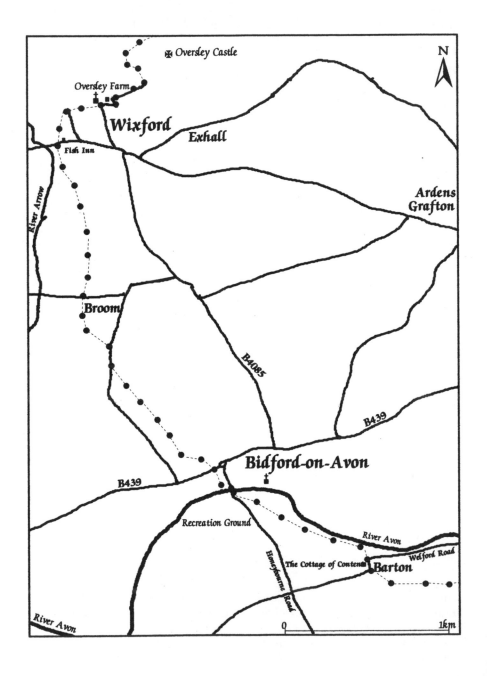

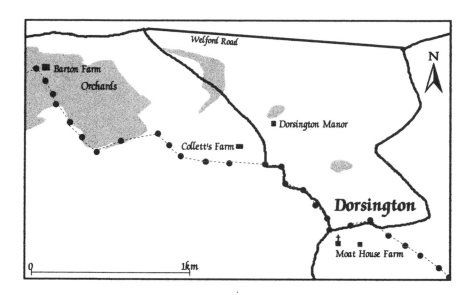

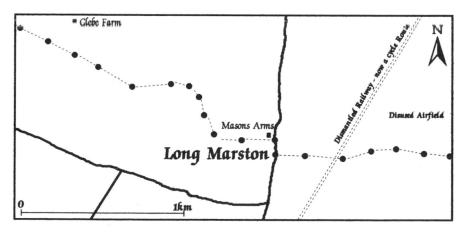

lightful river scene as you cross the River Avon.

Once over the bridge, go left over a stile to proceed diagonally in a south-east direction over a series of fields with the occasional stile. Soon the path reaches the banks of the Avon for a lovely short stretch of riverside walking with a weir to the left

ahead. Follow the path as it goes right over a stile to arrive at the B4085 in the hamlet of Barton. The Cottage of Content pub is on the right. Continue ahead past the pub, crossing the road to walk the pavement. In 100 metres the road bends sharp right but you continue ahead up a wide, hedged track which

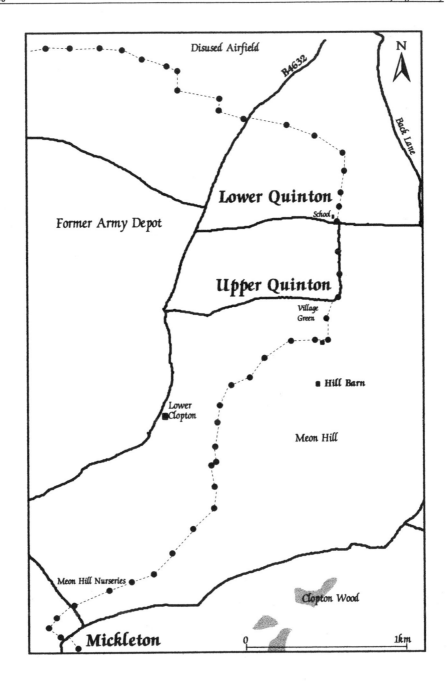

climbs, arcing left, to pass by an old fruit packing station and to reach Barton Farm.

Go right in front of the buildings and follow the left field hedge for some 500 metres. Reach and go through a hedge gap. Here, go left for some 250 metres then go right by a field hedge, crossing over a small brook on a path which arcs left to reach a track. Continue ahead with Collett's Farm to your left and you will emerge on the corner of the lane via a gate. Go right and walk this quiet lane for about 750 metres to reach a road junction in the village of Dorsington. At the junction, go left to pass by the village church and to cross a stream bridge. Go right over a stile to commence a 1½-mile (2.3km) walk over a series of fields and stiles by the side of the stream. Initially you will walk in a south-easterly direction; then later arc left then right (at a footbridge). Finally, bear left at a stile and go over two further stiles to arrive in Long Marston village near to the Mason's Arms pub.

Go right along the road for 50 metres then cross over to go left into a narrow, hedged lane. Keep straight ahead (south-east) to cross over a dismantled railway (now a cycle track) to a farm track leading through a gate. Just after passing two small lakes/ponds, leave the track via a gate and continue to the right of the field hedge over a series of fields. In about 750 metres, bear right at a field end then left at the next field corner to go through a gate. At the next field end go right over a stile then through a gate and over a final stile to the Campden road.

Cross the road and continue south-west over three more fields with stiles and a gate. Bear right (south) on a clear path over two more fields to arrive in a school playing field. Proceed by the hedge to the left of the school buildings to reach a gate leading to the main street in the village of Lower Quinton. Cross the road then go left then immediately right to walk a lane into the village of Upper Quinton. An 800-metre lane walk will bring you to the large village green where a bench seat marks the end of the Centenary Way.

Upper Quinton to Blockley

Distance: 10 miles (16km)

Duration: 5½ hours

Terrain: Mainly easy walking through delightful Cotswold countryside. Take time to explore Broad Campden and Chipping Campden.

From the village green in Upper Quinton, continue south along the road towards **Meon Hill** but bear right over a stile to enter a field to the right of a cottage. Follow the clear waymarks on a path which arcs left, generally following the hill contour to the west of Meon Hill and going over a series of fields and stiles. In about 1¼ miles (2km), the path arcs right to go over a footbridge and a further stile. It passes between derelict glasshouses before reaching the B4632 in Mickleton.

Cross over the B4632 and go over the stile opposite, aiming for a further stile in the field's far left corner. When over the stile, go immediately left and proceed between shop buildings to reach the B4632 once again, near the centre of the village of **Mickleton**. Go left for 25 metres then cross the road to walk the lane opposite, which soon reaches a kissing gate. The lane becomes a footpath and bears right by a ha-ha wall to go through a further kissing gate into the churchyard of St Lawrence's Church.

Exit the churchyard via its main gate then go left through a gate into pastureland. Cross the field and go through a further gate immediately opposite to walk the clear path in and along the edge of a small copse. Shortly after the path bends right, go right over a stile and ascend the slope of Baker's Hill to reach a gate in the field's top corner. Cross the road and go up the steps opposite to go over a stile. Bear right and walk the top edge of woodland. The path enters the superb woodland then emerges into a field. Continue to the right of the field hedge until you reach a barn. Here go left then right to join a lane. Walk this lane for the next 800 metres, passing by Starveall Farm (on the right) and Longlands Farm (on your left). You will arrive at a T-junction with Furze Lane.

Go right and walk Furze Lane for 350 metres, then go left down the drive to Mickleton Hills Farm. Pass in front of the farm complex, bearing right to cross over a railway tunnel with woodland on your left as you descend to go through a further gate into a cultivated field. Go right and continue on the path to the left of the field hedge, ascending gently to the top of the rise. Pause here to enjoy a fine retrospective view as well as the view of Chipping Campden ahead.

Proceed to pass to the left of school playing fields then go right over a stile to walk a fenced path in front of the impressive school complex. The path bends left. You will go through a metal kissing gate, cross the school drive and then descend a narrow path to the B4035 in

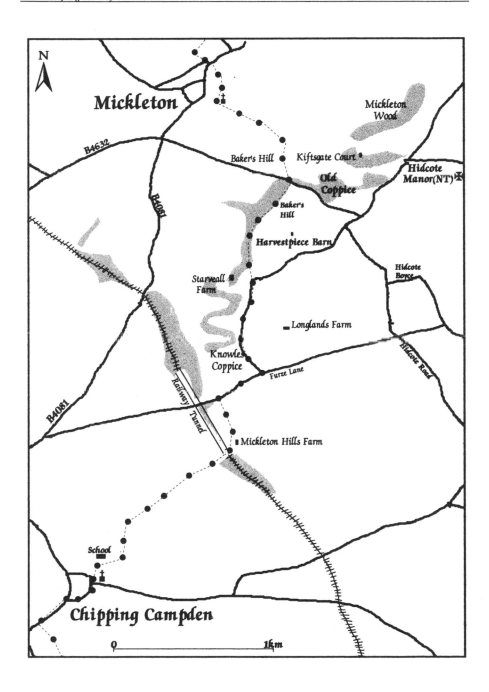

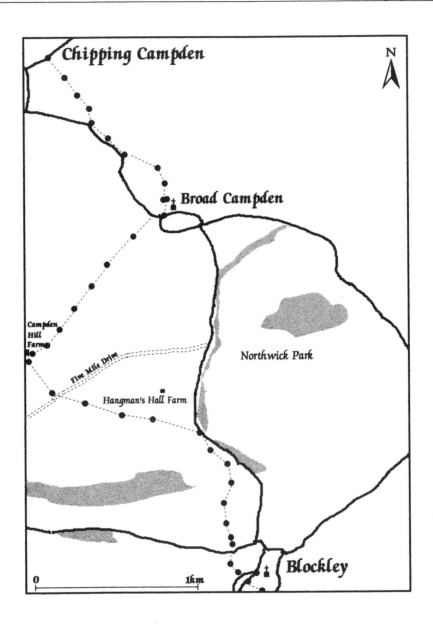

Chipping Campden. Cross the one-way street and go left to walk the pavement past St James's Church and the old almshouses and to arrive at the High Street in the town.

Go left and walk this beautiful street pausing to admire its many fine Cotswold buildings and its old Market Hall and its impressive Woolstaplers Hall. When you reach the Noel Arms Pub, go left through the pubs archway entrance and continue ahead between attractive houses onto a road and then still ahead to walk a hedged/walled footpath to the left of tennis courts. You will emerge onto the Chipping Campden to Blockley road, where you go left through a gateway to walk the path to the left of the road-hedge. This pleasing stretch of walking veers away from the road then bends right to reach a kissing gate at the entrance to **Broad Campden.**

Follow the waymarkers which will lead you down to the road by the attractive village church, Now go right and just around the corner you will arrive at The Bakers Arms Inn. Go left opposite to the inn passing through a gate to the right of a wall and continue in a south-west direction walking diagonally over a large field aiming for a stile in its far right-hand corner. Go over the stile and continue south-west ascending to the top of the field and passing to the right of a small fenced area. Now bear left and walk the clear path by the hill wall/fence going over a couple of stiles and then arcing right to reach a small hand gate with Campden Hill Farm ahead.

Go through the gate and proceed to the left of the farm buildings to reach the farm lane via a second gate. Go left and walk this fine Cotswold stone lane as it ascends south-east to reach Five Mile Drive. Walk through the trees of the drive and continue on the lane to the left of a hedge – you will soon see Hangman's Hall Farm to your left. You will pass through a small copse and go right through a gate into a field. Now go left and walk the left field edge, descending steeply to go through a gate by a spring stream. Cross the stream and ascend the hill opposite aiming for a gap between the 2nd and 3rd trees on the brow of the hill ahead and to go over a stile.

Continue by the field fence to the next stile then descend a cultivated field with the beauty of the village of Blockley coming into sight. You will go over a final stile to the left of a row of houses onto a road. Cross over the road and walk the lane opposite until you reach a small green. Now go left and descend the road into the centre of **Blockley** emerging near the general stores with a fine view of the church ahead. The small car park (with toilets) may be reached by going left along the road or by going past the general stores, through the churchyard and bearing left.

Blockley to Bourton-on-the-Water

Distance: 12 miles (19km)

Duration: 6½ hours

Terrain: Mainly easy walking but with some undulations.

From the car park in Blockley, walk through the churchyard and bear right to a street near to the general stores. Here, go left. Just after passing The Crown Inn, go left again to descend to the B4479. At the road junction go left, then go right on a track which leads over stiles to pass a fishpond and to cross a farm track. Proceed up the hill to the right of Park Farm and in 400 metres go over a stile to a tree-lined track. Pause here and enjoy a superb view back to Blockley before going left and walking the track for 100 metres. Now go right through a gate and walk to the left of a hedge until you reach a lane via a further gate.

Cross the lane and enter Park Plantation via a gate. Descend a clear path to the right of the wall to Batsford Park. This pleasant stretch of woodland walking continues through Century Plantation before bearing right and then left to join an estate road. This follows a south-east direction and goes over a couple of stiles towards the lodge house to Batsford Park.

Go over the stile to the right of the lodge and walk to a further stile in the field corner. Now go right (south-west), aiming for a stile that takes you onto the park drive. Here go left and walk the drive to reach the busy A44. At the A44 go right and continue for 650 metres into **Bourton-on-the-Hill.** Cross the road with care to walk the road to the left of the village church and to bear right around the back of the church.

Now go left on a walled track between houses to go through a gate to beautiful, open pastureland. Proceed in a southerly direction, going over a stile and passing through a pair of kissing gates to enter the parkland of **Sezincote House.** This delightful stretch of walking will take you through trees for a view of the Duckery Lake to your left, with a magnificent view of Sezincote House to your right. Continue in the same direction. Go through a gate and up a field to the left of trees to go through a further gate to a farm lane (there is a cattle grid to the right).

Cross over the lane and proceed ahead on a path that becomes a track through the trees of Gold Barrows Copse. Go through a small, heavy, iron gate to open pastureland. Walk the Way path to the right of the field hedge, with pleasing views of **Moreton in Marsh** to your left. Pass to the right of Manor Farm to reach the road on the outskirts of **Longborough.**

Go left at the road and walk into the village, passing by The Coach and Horses public house. Go right by the village school to walk a lane going south. Shortly after arcing left the lane becomes a pleasant track called

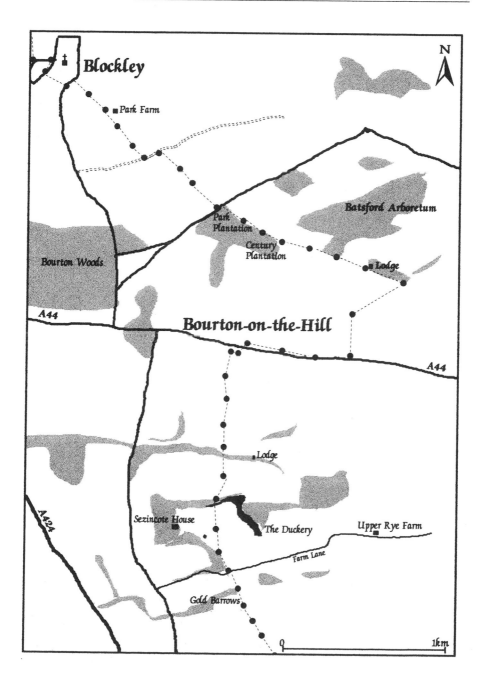

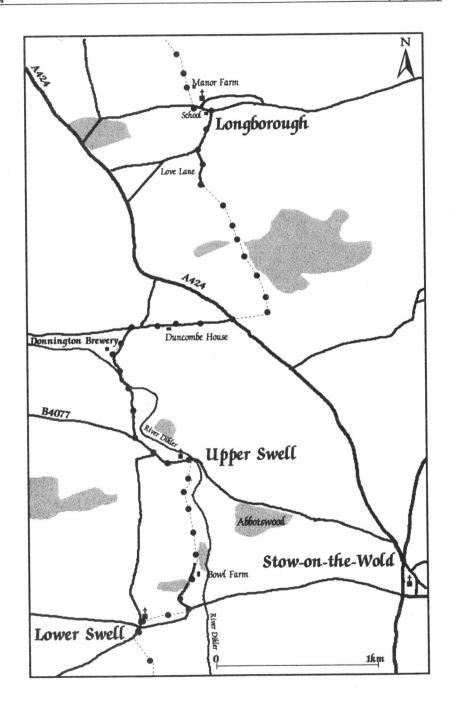

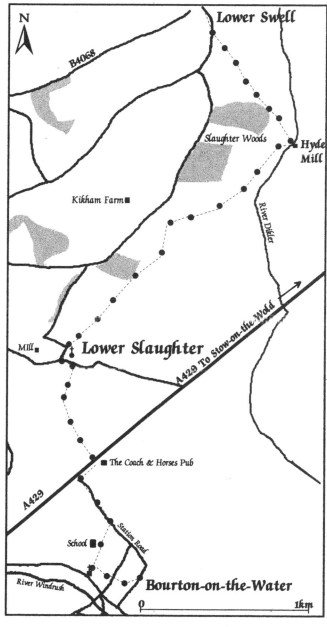

through the gate, bear right off the track to continue on the Way and go over a stile to reach open land once again. Continue on the path to the right of woodland, going over a couple of stiles. In about 900 metres you will reach a junction of paths. Now go right and walk a hedged track up to the A424.

Cross the A424 and descend the lane opposite, passing by Dunscombe House then bearing left at a road junction to descend past **Donnington Brewery**. Cross over the River Swell and climb to the A4077 on the edge of **Upper Swell**. Go left along the pavement of the B4077 and in about 400 metres, when just past the church, cross the road and go through a hand gate to continue south along the Way. Follow the clear signs over a series of fields with

'Love Walk Lane' and leads through a farm gate. Immediately after going the River Swell close by on the left. You will go through several kissing gates, stiles and squeeze stiles, before going over a stile and on to a lane near to Bowl Farm.

Go right and walk the lane past Bowl Farm and the attractive Lady's Well. Just before the lane bends right (near the turn to the Abbotswood Estate), go right over a stile and ascend a field, aiming for a stile set to the left of **Lower Swell** Church. Go over the stile to a road in the village – on the hill to your left you will see **Stow-on-the-Wold**. Now go left and descend over the road junction and the B4068 to a lane leading towards the Slaughters.

Walk the pavement for some 200 metres then bear left down a track that leads to open fields. After going through a gate you will walk a wide, fenced track going south-east. It then bears south once again, going over stiles to reach Hyde Farm. Although the Way goes to the right of the buildings, spare time to see the old mill from its bridge to the left of the buildings – it makes a delightful scene.

Return to the Way path and walk along the farm drive. One hundred metres after it bends right, go left through a gate and into pastureland. Your clear path continues in a general south-east direction for the next $1\frac{1}{4}$ miles (2km), going over several stiles. Initially the path is close to the River Dikler, then it passes woodlands. Eventually, it follows to the left of a hedge to arrive in **Lower Slaughter** by the village cricket pavilion. Exit the playing field area via a small gate and walk through a housing estate to reach a road. Here go left to pass by the church and to reach the main road in this attractive Cotswold village. (To visit the superb old mill, go right for about 200 metres then right again.)

Go left and cross the road to walk by the side of the River Eye for about 75 metres. Then go right to walk a wide pathway by the side of a stream. After passing through gates the tarmac path veers south-east over open land to reach the busy A429 opposite to the Coach and Horses pub. Cross the road with great care and go right along the pavement for about 100 metres. Go left into Station Road on the outskirts of **Bourton-on-the-Water**.

In about 400 metres, cross the road and go right to walk a wide paved area, passing by schools with the town church to your right. In about 350 metres go left, following the Way marks on a path at the back of houses. Cross a road and then go left to arrive in the Station Road Pay and Display car park.

The Heart of England Way: South to North

The River Avon at Barton, near Bidford-on-Avon

Bourton-on-the-Water to Blockley

Distance: 12 miles (19km)

Duration: 6½ hours

Terrain: Mainly easy walking but with some undulations.

Place names: throughout the route descriptions, wherever a place name appears in bold within the walks, you will find a detailed description of the place in the final section of this book.

Leave **Bourton-on-the-Water** on the footpath going towards the town centre from the Station Road car park, but bear right at the back of houses. In about 200 metres go right and pass by school buildings on the way to Station Road. Here, go left to reach the main A429 Fosse Way road. Now

go right for about 100 metres, passing by The Coach and Horses pub. Cross the road to a large kissing gate that leads into pastureland.

Follow the clear path over the fields, going through two further kissing gates to walk by the River Eye into the very attractive village of **Lower Slaughter**. Here a small detour to visit the Old Mill is worth while. At the village road, go left along the side of the River Eye for about 75 metres then go right past the church, following the Way

The River Windrush at Bourton-on-the-Water

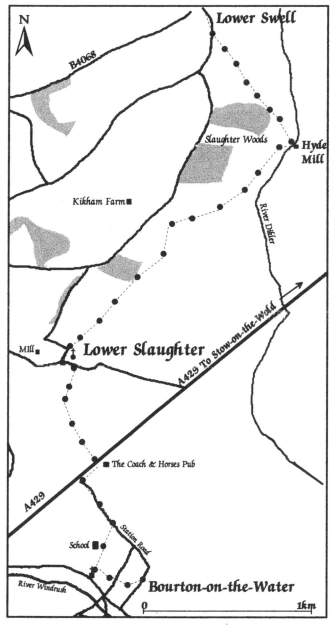

of the Old Mill by walking by the River Eye for 250 metres then going right to walk a narrow footpath by the side of the mill. Pause to visit the museum and gift shop – the ice creams are highly recommended. Continue up the lane, going past the sign for the Warden's Way, and walk among the attractive village cottages to reach a T-junction. Here, go right for about 250 metres then go left.

Proceed through a housing estate to a small gate. Continue along the back of a cricket pavilion, passing the village cricket pitch to walk with a hedge on your right. In about 100 metres, go right through a hedge gap to the other side of the hedge and continue along the left-hand edge of the field for about 400 metres, eventually with

waymarks. Alternatively, you could take time to see the fine waterwheel

trees on your left. Cross a stile/bridge to a gateway then proceed over the

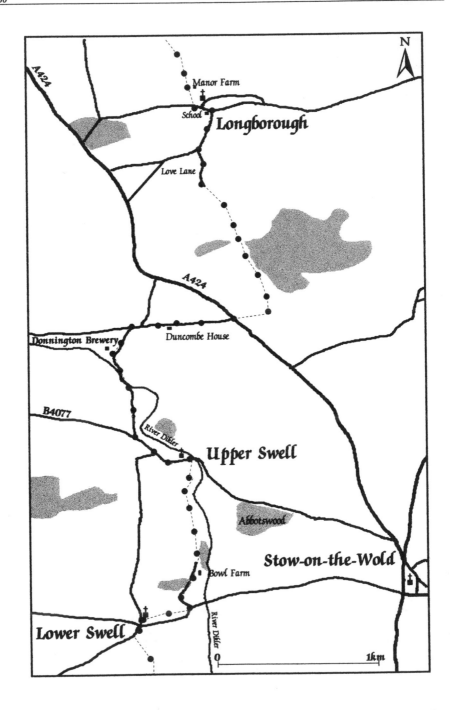

N

A424

Manor Farm

School

Longborough

Love Lane

A424

Donnington Brewery

Duncombe House

B4077

River Dikler

Upper Swell

Abbotswood

Stow-on-the-Wold

Bowl Farm

Lower Swell

River Dikler

0   1km

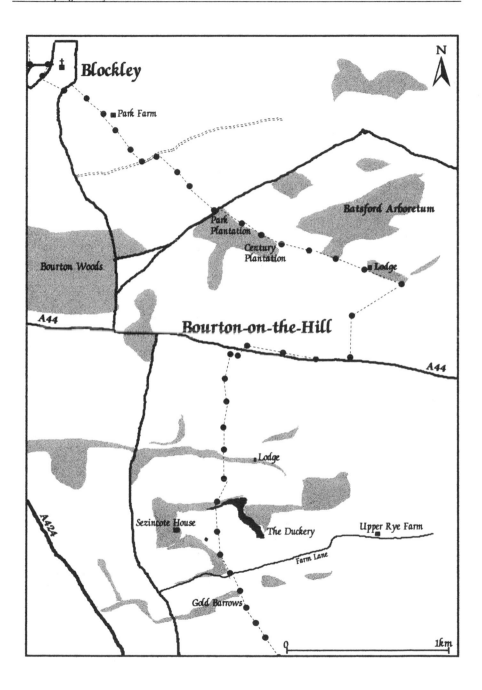

next field to a squeeze stile. Your route now keeps you near the River Dickler.

Continue along the path, over a stile and through a swing gate and then proceed over a stone bridge, aiming generally to a further bridge near Hyde Mill. After crossing the bridge, go right and walk to the left of the mill buildings. Cross the next field to a gate and bridge with Slaughter Woods on the left. The path becomes a wide grass track between wired (electric?) fences for about 800 metres. Nether Swell Manor is passed on your far right as you walk the grass track to reach a gate and a stone-walled track.

At the end of the walled track, go right on to a lane that leads into **Lower Swell**. There is a large farm complex on your right and you will pass by several attractive Cotswold cottages. **Stow-on-the-Wold** is on the hill to the right. Bear right into the centre of Lower Swell then veer left to the road junction at the village centre. Go ahead up a metalled road towards the superb village church with its three visible bells. Go over a stile to the right of the church then veer right across the village field to a further stile on to the lane near the main entrance to Abbotswood Estate.

Do not enter the estate road but go left along the lane, passing by Lady's Well on your left. You soon pass Bowl Farm on your right. Go through a kissing gate to a path over pastureland. Follow the path over several fields and through kissing gates to reach a metal squeeze stile. Cross the next field to a second metal

squeeze stile and walk along the bottom hedge of this field to a small gate to the B4077 in **Upper Swell**.

Here, go left and walk along the B4077 for about 400 metres, passing the village church, then go right onto the Longborough road, going north. Proceed along the road as it descends past a water treatment works on the right, then cross over the bridge over the River Dickler. Continue along the road as it climbs to pass the famous **Donnington Brewery** on your left.

In about 200 metres go right at a lane junction for a steeper ascent. Pass a cattery and Dunscombe House to reach the A424 Evesham to Stow-on-the-Wold road. Cross the A424 and continue along a clear, hedged track for about 300 metres before going left over a stile to descend a field with woods on your right. You will cross over two footbridges/stiles, aiming north-northwest over a series of fields and stiles and keeping some mature oak trees on your right. The path soon reaches a stile that takes you onto a well-worn track. Here, go left and go through a gate into Love Walk Lane. Stroll up into the little-known but very attractive Cotswold village of **Longborough**. Bear right to walk into the village centre and then go left at the T-junction (the village school will be on the left corner) to pass The Coach and Horses public house, also on your left.

From The Coach and Horses, veer left for about 50 metres then go right to walk between allotments and the churchyard to reach a kissing gate into fields. Proceed along this waymarked path, passing Manor

Farm on the right and walking the right-hand edge of several fields, always enjoying the pleasing view to your right. Soon you will go through a kissing gate to walk the edge of Gold Barrows copse and to arrive at a small, heavy, iron gate. Reach a farm lane by a 5-bar gate near a cattle grid (on the left). Cross the lane and continue ahead through a further gate, initially keeping close to the woodland on your left. Veer to the left of a mid-field tree to diagonally cross the field to yet another gate – this one with a water trough adjacent. Proceed over the next field, pausing to look to your left to enjoy a fine view of the magnificent building of **Sezingcote House**.

As you approach a gate over a stream, pause to view The Duckery lake to your right. Continue over the estate grounds, passing through two kissing gates and crossing further fields and stiles. There is a fine view over **Moreton-in-the-Marsh** to the right. Soon you will reach a gate that leads to a narrow lane – follow this lane into the village of **Bourton-on-the-Hill**, passing next to its church to reach the busy A44, Broadway to Moreton-in-the-Marsh road.

At the A44, go right and descend the footpath for about 600 metres, then go left into the driveway of Batsford Arboretum, Falconry and Garden Centre. Proceed up the driveway for 350 metres then go right over a stile and head in a north-east direction to the next field corner. Go left for 250 metres to emerge on the driveway by the lodge. Go over the stile opposite and climb the hill to a

further stile before going left on a clear track through trees. As the track bends to the left, go right up a path into the trees to reach a gateway. Here go left and walk by the side of Batsford Park wall on the right-hand edge of Century and Park Plantations. Eventually you will reach a lane. Cross and continue through the gate opposite to reach a stile. Ahead there is a good view of Blockley and the surrounding area. Continue to the right of a low wall over two fields. You then reach a stile that takes you onto a wide, tree-lined track.

Go left along this tree-lined track for about 100 metres then go right over a stile to descend a field. Aim for a further stile set to the left of Park Farm. As you descend the field you will be mesmerised by a superb view of Blockley and the surrounding countryside – a typical Cotswold view. Proceed down to the next field, where you will pass a fishpond on the left and then go over another stile that leads to a track. Go down this track into the very attractive Cotswold village of **Blockley**.

Blockley to Upper Quinton

Distance: 10 miles (16km)

Duration: 5½ hours

Terrain: Mainly easy walking through delightful Cotswold countryside.

Leave **Blockley** by exiting the churchyard at its rear and going left up Bell Bank into Bucks End. Proceed along Chapel Lane then cross Greenway Road. Climb by houses to a stile, then cross a cultivated field to go through a gap in its far hedge to reach a stile into a fenced enclosure. Proceed over the stile to a second stile and into a field with five large trees in a row on its brow. Aim to walk between the second and third trees (from the left) and descend to go through a farm gate over a stream.

From the gate, climb the next field, going to the right of a large oak tree. Walk up by the right-hand hedge to go through two gates set either side of a small 'bull' paddock. Proceed right through a gap in the hedge of the small beech plantation near to the Blockley to Broad Campden road, but then veer left to walk a path by the left-hand edge of a field with Hangman's Hall Farm on your right.

The path soon joins a stone farm drive, ascending north-west by the hedge to reach and cross Five Mile Drive before descending once again as it veers left towards Campden Hill Farm. Immediately before the farm, go right through a small gate and follow the path to a second gate set to the right (east) of the farm buildings. Bear right and climb to the top of the ridge. Continue in a generally

north-east direction over several stiles, walking by the fence for about 700 metres. Then descend gently to a gate by a wall, which is situated almost opposite the Baker's Arms Inn in the very pretty village of Broad Campden.

Go right along the road then left just before the village church to enter an alleyway of attractive period cottages and to pass Maidenwall Cottage on your right. Leave Broad Campden by a kissing gate near the cottage. There is a fine view over **Chipping Campden,** with its church standing proud on the hill ahead. Proceed over the field, bearing left at a path junction to soon walk by the side of the hedge by the side of the Chipping Campden to Broad Campden road. In about 300 metres go left onto the road, and almost immediately go right into George Lane to pass Chipping Campden Tennis Club and playing fields on your left. By walking this lane you will arrive at the back of the Noel Arms public house in Chipping Campden. Enter the town through a gateway to reach the High Street near to the Woolstapler's Hall and Museum.

Go right along the High Street, passing by the superb market hall on your left. In about 300 metres go right into Church Street, passing some fine Cotswold almshouses on the left. Walk up Church Street towards

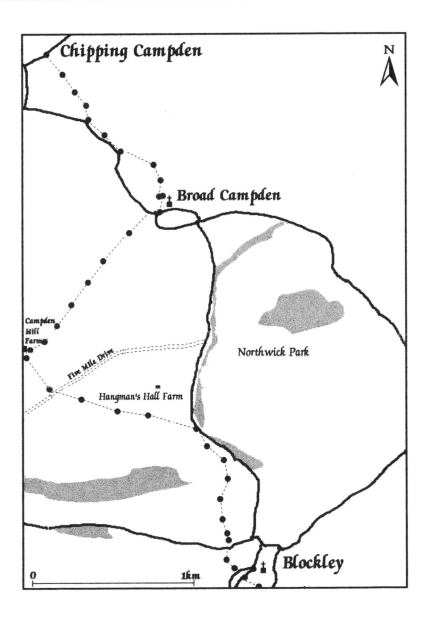

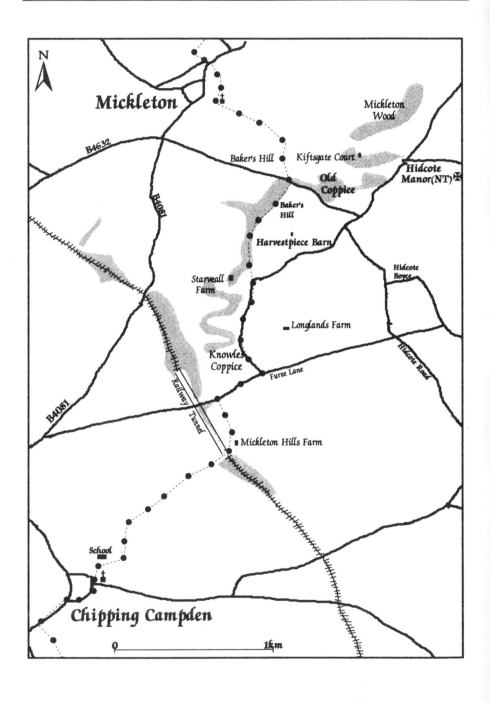

an impressive gateway then follow the road as it bends to the left of St James's Church.

Continue past the B4035 (Shipston-on-Stour road) and in about 50 metres cross the road to go right up a pleasant, narrow path which leads between houses to arrive on the drive to a large school. Cross the drive and go through the metal kissing gate opposite, bearing initially left and then right to walk a hedged/fenced footpath in front of the school buildings. At the footpath end, go over a stile and go left to walk a path by the side of the fence/hedge to the school playing fields.

Proceed by the hedge of a large field, gradually descending towards woodland. Go left through a gate immediately before the woods and walk by the side of the trees to reach and walk in front of Mickleton Hills Farm. Continue up the farm drive and go right at the junction to walk along Furze Lane for some 350 metres then go left along a lane. You will pass Knowles Coppice and Starveal Farm on your left. As the lane bends to the right (just after some farm buildings), go left and then right to walk to the left of the hedge through a stretch of very pleasant trees on the lip of Blake's Hill. Soon you will emerge from the woodland to walk to the right of the trees. In about 200 metres, go left over a stile and descend a bank to reach a lane. Cross over this lane, pausing by the gate opposite to enjoy a fine view through the trees of the village of **Mickleton** set in the valley below. Go through the gate and descend the field, aiming for a stile in its bottom left-hand corner. Go over the stile and bear left to walk by the hedge. Proceed through two gates to arrive in Mickleton village near to the church.

Walk in front of the church, bearing right through the churchyard to a kissing gate at the back of the church. Go through this gate and walk by the side of a ha-ha at the back of houses to reach a further kissing gate that leads to the B4632, Stratford to Chipping Campden road. Go left at the road. Just before a road that goes off to the right, cross over to walk a passageway to the right of the butcher's shop on the corner. Proceed to go over a stile in the far right-hand corner of the field at the rear of the shop. From here aim north east to go over a further stile in the far hedge and to cross the B4632 to a farm track. This leads between the dilapidated glasshouses of Meon Hill Nurseries.

The track eventually veers to the left to go over a stile and cross the next field on a clear path that goes over a footbridge. Follow the path over a series of fields and stiles that hug the contour of Meon Hill – such a shame that one cannot walk over the top of the hill. Keep to the contour level on the path that bears right to pass to the left of a house on the entry to the village of Upper Quinton.

Upper Quinton to Alcester

Distance: 11½ miles (18km)

Duration: 6½ hours

Terrain: Mainly easy walking through pleasant rural countryside. The stretch leading up to Alcester is particularly attractive.

Pass the fine green as you leave the village of Upper Quinton and bear right to walk the lane into the neighbouring village of Lower Quinton. Go over the road in the village and through a gate into the school grounds. Walk to the right of the school buildings to go over a stile into a cultivated field. Cross the field to a further stile/footbridge, which you go over. Bear left to walk by the field hedge over three further fields to reach a stile onto the B4632 Campden road.

Cross the road, go over the stile opposite and walk by the left-hand field edge. Go right at the field end to go over a mid-field gate. Proceed, bearing initially right then left to walk over several fields. Follow the waymarkers as you walk to the left of Long Marston Airfield. You will pass through a couple of gates to arrive on a farm track which soon crosses over a dismantled railway (now a cycleway) to walk a lane into the village of Long Marston and to reach its main road. Cross over the Long Marston road and go right for about 50 metres. Go left before the Masons Arms pub, proceeding behind cottages over a stile into open fields. Cross the field and go right over two further stiles to walk by the right-hand edge of the next field. Go right over another stile to walk by the hedge over three fur-

ther fields and to reach a footbridge over a small stream. Cross the footbridge and go diagonally left across the next field and then walk by the side of the stream. Go over three stiles to reach a final stile to a lane leading into the village of Dorsington.

Go left into the village, passing the church on your left to reach a road junction. Here, go right and walk the lane for almost 750 metres. At the second bend in the lane, go ahead through a gate to a track with Collett's Farm on your right. Proceed through a second gate and follow the waymarkers as the track initially proceeds to the right of the hedge and then continues on the left of the hedge to reach a large fruit orchard.

In about 250 metres, go right to walk a field edge by the side of orchards and to approach Barton Farm. Go to the left of the buildings, bearing left and soon right by the left side of the hedge. As the fruit packing station comes into view, go left at the field corner to walk to the right of the packing station buildings. Continue on the track as it bears to the right and gently descends into the village of Barton.

At the road go right and then go ahead through a gate to the right of the Cottage of Content pub. Walk a wide track down to the River Avon.

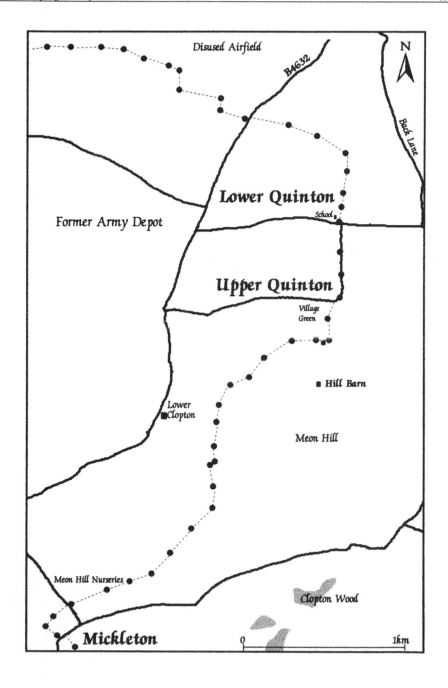

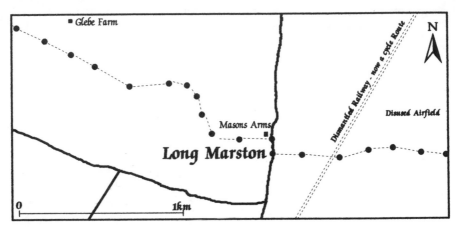

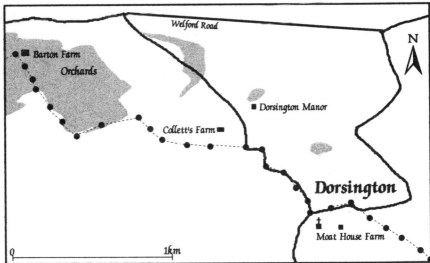

At the river go left along the river-bank, going over three stiles to reach open fields with the town of **Bidford-on-Avon** appearing to your right. Diagonally cross the large field, going over a mid-field stile and aligning for a further stile sited by the Bidford Bridge over the river.

Take care crossing over the busy, narrow bridge then go left along the shopping street. In about 50 metres, just past the Frog and Bullrush pub, cross the road and proceed up an enclosed footpath between buildings. Ascend the path as it passes between a second block of buildings then go left along a residential road. Proceed up this road which arcs to the right and in about 400 metres arrives at open land. Cross the open area and continue on the footpath, going to the right of more houses and emerg-

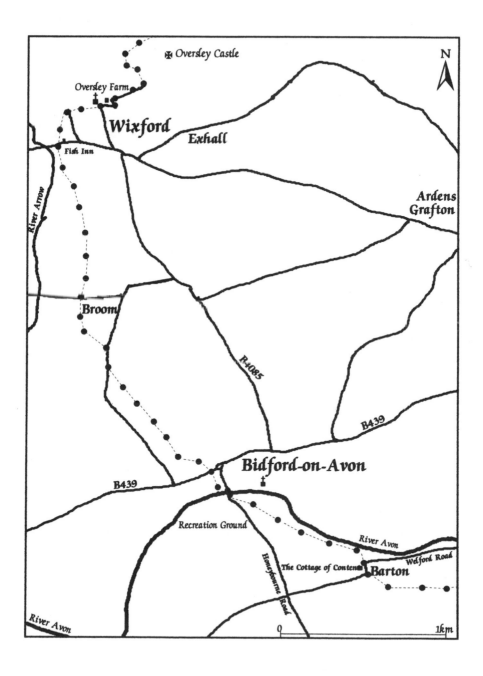

ing to go right along the Broom to Bidford Road. Proceed up and across the road to go over the former railway bridge. Just over the top of the bridge, go left and descend some steps to walk a field at the back of houses in the village of Broom.

Proceed in a northerly direction by the side of a hedge across a playing field. Emerge on a road near the Broom Tavern Inn. Cross the road and continue on the signed path to go over a stile to open fields. Proceed over a series of stiles and gates, passing Moor Hall on the left. In about 600 metres you will walk close to the River Arrow before reaching a road opposite the Fish Inn in Wixford.

Cross the road and proceed through the pub car park to go through a gate and past caravans. Continue over a stile, walking to the left of a new house and eventually the premises of Eurogas. Continue on the path as it goes right by Eurogas and then passes to the right of the attractive Wixford Church to reach a lane. Here, go right then immediately left to walk the lane opposite, which goes to the right of Oversley Farm and then gently ascends towards Oversley Castle set upon the hill ahead. **Do not** enter the main drive to the castle as this is private property, but continue along a track which curves left by trees below the castle and passes by a farm cottage and farm buildings on the left. Continue along the good stone track as it bends to the left and climbs towards two large grain silos by the farm buildings of Lower Oversley Lodge.

Proceed to the right of the silos and bear right to descend towards a footbridge over the Alcester bypass on the busy A46. Go over the stile and cross the bridge, then walk the pretty Primrose Lane into the village of Oversley Green. At the T-junction in this attractive village, go right for 125 metres then go left over a bridge over the river. This takes you to the Old Stratford Road and into the town of **Alcester**.

Cross the road and walk through an attractive riverside park to reach Malt Mill Lane. Go right up the cobbled lane to pass between some beautifully renovated almshouses and to reach the Main Street opposite the church in Alcester. Go right and walk past the church and the impressive town hall.

Alcester to Rowington

Distance: 12½ miles (20km)

Duration: 7 hours

Terrain: Mainly easy walking through pleasant rural countryside.

From the town hall in **Alcester**, proceed up the pavement towards Great Alne. Go over the bridge over the River Arrow, passing the Greig Memorial Hall on your left and passing the turning to the Arden Forest Industrial Estate also on the left. In about 100 metres, go left up a hedged path to go over a stile into open fields. Ascend the clear path, pausing to enjoy the view of Alcester from the trig point (66m). Continue to go over two stiles, an old railway bridge and a further stile at the bridge end. Proceed up the side of the hedge to go over a stile to the left (in about 100 metres) and then to walk the other

side of the hedge to go over another stile.

Continue on the clear track by the hedge to go through a gate to Coughton Fields Lane. Here, go left for 25 metres then cross the lane to go over a stile on the right and climb the slope to a further stile in the top left-hand corner of the field. This takes you to a hedged track. Cross the track and emerge from the trees to walk a clear path to the right that follows the hedge. In about 300 metres, go through a gap in the hedge to walk its far side. The path arcs to the left. Go over a stile and walk north-east to a further stile to the right of New End

Primrose Lane, Oversley Green, near Alcester

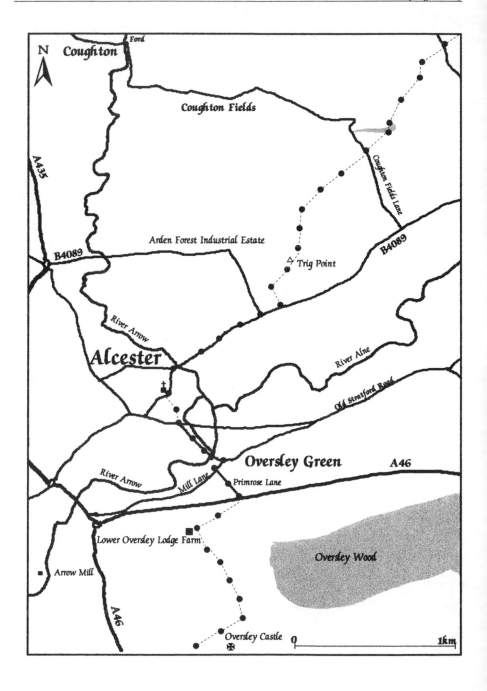

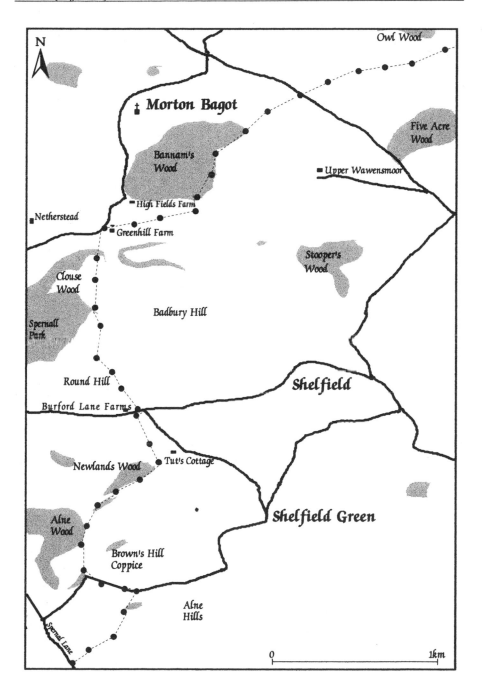

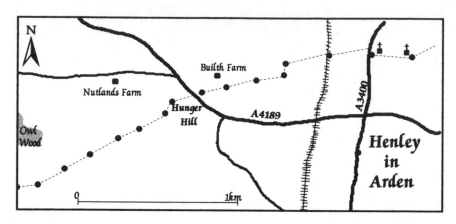

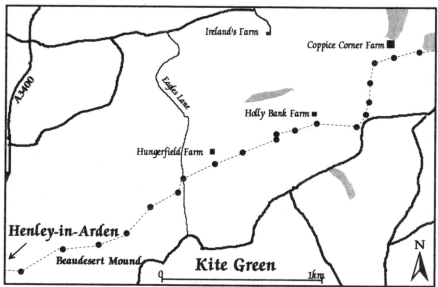

Cottages. Go over this and you are on a lane.

Cross the lane, veering to the left to enter and walk a farm drive opposite. In about 400 metres, go left over a stile and up two fields to reach and go over a stile. Here, go left and walk the lane for about 400 metres then, as the road bends left, go right over a cattle grid/gate and proceed north to

walk a track to the right of Alne Wood (full of bluebells in May). Proceed up the track to the right of a barn and walk the edge of Burnett Brake, then continue to the right of New-lands Wood (another bluebell wood), going over a stile in the far right-hand corner of the large field.

Walk the next field, aiming to-wards a gate in the far left-hand cor-

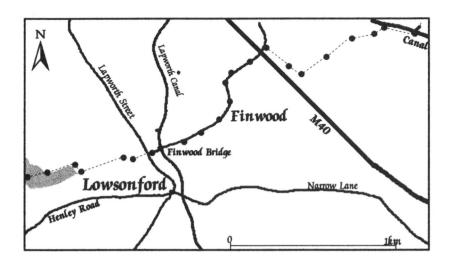

ner to take you to Burford Lane. Go right for about 75 metres, walking by some very attractive cottage gardens, and then go left up a track to go over a stile. Walk by the field hedge over three fields and stiles, initially with Round Hill on your left. At the third stile, proceed around the hedge ahead to go through a hedge gap just in front of Clouse Wood. From the gap aim north and cross a large cultivated field, proceeding to the left of a hedge. You will go over two stiles and then descend through an attractive copse before ascending the next field to go through a metal gate to a lane. Here go right. As the lane bends left, go right through gates to walk between buildings and into a long field. Here you will walk past a pond on your left with High Fields Farm sited beneath Bannam's Wood. Proceed over a stile to reach a hand gate by trees and then go left. Go up and into woodland. Reach a gate and then walk a permissive path to the

right of the wood. There is a fine view over the Wootton Wawen countryside.

Continue over a stile at the wood end then make a steep but attractive descent by the field edge. Go over a stile and cross a lane. Walk the path opposite as it continues to the right of the hedge for some 400 metres then veers north-east across the field to go over a mid-hedge stile. Go ahead and up the next field to go over a further stile to the left of a water tank. Proceed diagonally over the next field to go over another stile in its far corner. Walk the path as it continues north-east to a footbridge and then climbs left to a stile into a fenced area. As you leave the fenced area, proceed ahead over an excellent brick stile to the left of a house and cross the A4189 to the stile opposite. Continue east-north-east over three more fields, going over a footbridge and then bearing left. In about 100 metres, go right to walk a fenced path with allotments to your right. Soon you will reach and go over a footbridge over the railway line at Henley-in-Arden. As you leave the railway station complex, go left and then right to walk a clear, hedged footpath that leads into the High Street (the A3400) in **Henley-in-Arden**. Cross the A3400 at the traffic lights and then go right to walk near the church. Go left immediately after the church buildings and walk an attractive road over a bridge. In about 100 metres go left by the church and ascend the steep path to go over the top of Beaudesert Mount, pausing to enjoy the pleasant views.

Walk the clear path as it continues over fine undulating land to go over a stile at its top end and then to proceed to the left of a hedge. In about 200 metres, go right over a stile and diagonally cross the next field to go over a further stile. Go left up a hedged track for 50 metres, and then go right to walk in a north-east direction. Cross a farm track with Hungerfield Farm on your left, then go over three further fields.

At the second stile bear left and then soon right to continue in a north-east direction to go to the front of Holly Bank Farm. Here the path veers east to reach the Henley road. Go left for about 60 metres then go left again (as the road bends right), passing through a gate to walk a clear track. In about 400 metres go over the bridge over a dismantled railway then go right through a gate near to Coppice Corner Farm. Proceed on the path that veers down towards the trees above the dismantled railway

and then arcs left to continue through trees. At the copse end go over a stile and proceed to the left of trees, going over a double stile and going right along a wide track. In about 50 metres go left and walk the signed path, proceeding over a stile to arrive at Lapworth Street near Lowsonford.

Cross over Lapworth Street and proceed up Mill Lane opposite, pausing on the bridge over the Lapworth Canal to watch the barges in action. Continue up Mill Lane for almost a mile as it passes through the hamlet of Finwood and goes over the noisy M40. On the other side of the M40 bridge, go right and walk a lane which runs parallel with the motorway for some 300 metres. At the brow of a cutting, go left and walk a track that in about 500 metres bends right to go by the side of and above the **Grand Union Canal**. Go left over Rowington Bridge to cross the canal. Go up a lane to reach the Old Warwick Road in Rowington. To the left opposite the church is the church car park.

Rowington to Meriden

Distance: 11¼ miles (18km)

Duration: 6 hours

Terrain: Easy walking through attractive Warwickshire countryside.

Leave Rowington by crossing the Old Warwick Road to go through the churchyard gate to the front of the church. Bear left to go over a stile at the back of the church and walk the footpath over several fields and stiles, proceeding in a north-north-east direction. Pass Quarry Farm on your right and a most attractive windmill conversion on the left to go through a gate to a village lane. Go left and walk the lane for some 450 metres, enjoying the sight of attractive houses. Then go right through a gate to the right of Lyons Farm and walk a clear track that passes to the left of Rowington Coppice.

The track goes north, curving gradually right as it passes through further gates. It reaches a kissing gate near the attractive church. Walk the path to the left of the church and you will emerge by the superb National Trust property of **Baddesley Clinton Hall**. Not far away is **Packington Hall**, another attractive National Trust property. Walk the lane with the hall on your left and then bear right through a gate to walk to the right of a fine bluebell copse. Proceed over the footbridge at the copse end and then go between attractive houses and over three stiles to Hay Wood Lane.

Go left and walk the lane for about 300 metres to reach Rising Lane. At the junction go right and then left, passing between stables of the former convent. Exit the complex through a gate and proceed over several fields and gates/stiles to arrive at the Birmingham road in Chadwick End.

Go left, cross the road and then go right between buildings and along a lane at the back of gardens. As you arrive on a housing estate, go right and then left to walk a path behind the houses. Go over a stile and climb towards Priest's Park Wood.

Walk the path through the wood to a stile at its far end. Here, veer right to diagonally cross a large field and to go over a further stile in its far corner. Go left and walk a track in a north-east direction, going over a footbridge and several stiles as the path curves left to a final stile onto Oldwich Lane. Go right for 80 metres then go left over a stile and walk the path over several fields and stiles for about 500 metres. Now go left for 90 metres then go right over a stile to continue on a clear track for a little over three-quarters of a mile – the track arcs to the right of Balsall Lodge Farm to arrive in Fen End road.

Cross the road and walk a path to the left of Gate Farm, crossing three fields to reach a junction of paths. Here, go right over a stile and aim north-east through attractive scenery. The black and white buildings of

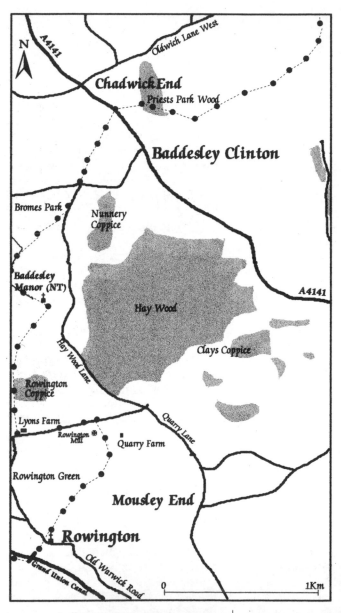

rejoin the lane. As an alternative, go right along Magpie Lane to walk past Magpie Farm and admire the superb half-timbered farmhouse – the lane circles to the left and soon arrives at Balsall Street. Go left and walk the pavement of the street for about 200 metres, then cross the road and go right over a stile to walk the path over a series of fields and a number of stiles and footbridges.

In about three-quarters of a mile the path becomes a lane and soon emerges at the A452. Here go left, taking care by this busy road. In 200 metres, cross the A452 and go right down Park Lane. In a further 250 metres, go left through a kissing gate and through trees to walk a

Magpie Farm are to the right. At Magpie Lane the Way goes left and then right over a stile to cross a field and to track in a north-east direction. Go through a further kissing gate near the lake at Berkswell Hall. Go right

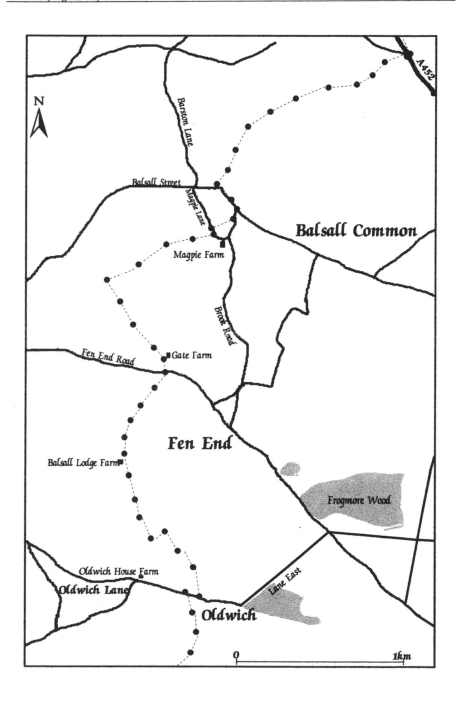

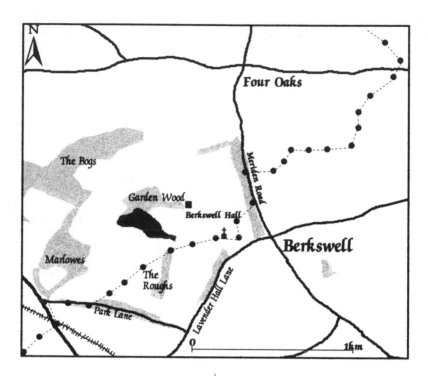

by the lake and proceed over a planked area with the hall to the left. Proceed through a gate and then a kissing gate to arrive near the splendid church in **Berkswell** – worth a stop and visit.

At the end of the churchyard go left through a kissing gate and then a gate to descend to a stile and further kissing gate onto the Meriden Road. Go left for about 200 metres, cross the road and then go right down a hedged track that bends right near Blend Hall Farm. The track goes east for about 350 metres before veering north-east over several fields to reach Back Lane.

Cross Back Lane and go over two stiles on a footpath that veers north-north-west over a number of fields and stiles. In about three-quarters of a mile the path reaches a lane. Go right then, shortly after going around a bend to the left, go left just past Meriden Church. Walk through the churchyard, where there is a pleasant view of Meriden appearing to the left.

Proceed along the path through three kissing gates and up steps to the B4102. Cross over the road, descend steps on the other side and emerge to the left of the inviting Queen's Head pub in Meriden.

Meriden to Kingsbury

Distance: 13½ miles (22km)

Duration: 7½ hours

Terrain: Easy walking. The reservoir at Shustoke is a good stopping place and you should allow time to explore.

From the Queen's Head pub in Meriden, proceed up Walsh Lane. In about 300 metres go left (with Village Farm on your left) to walk a narrow lane which in a further 400 metres walk dips beneath the main A45 Birmingham to Coventry road. Continue along the lane into Eaves Green.

In the village you will pass by a caravan site and then go left over a stile to a track which leads to Meriden Shafts. Proceed over a second stile then walk over two further fields and enter woodland over a further stile. Walk the path through the woods and go over a stile at its end. Now continue left then right on a clear track. Walk by the hedge in three fields and go over a stile to Harvest Hill Lane in Hollyberry End.

Go left and walk the lane for about 300 metres then, where the lane bends left, go right over a stile to diagonally cross a field to a stile/footbridge in its far left corner. Continue by walking the track on the edge of Birchley Hays Wood, then aim to go over a stile set to the left of Hayes Hall Farm ahead..

Go left along the Fillongley road and then right over a small, cultivated field, proceeding over a stile and walking to the left of a hedge. At the field corner go right over a stile and continue along a clear path going

north over a series of fields and stiles. Go over a footbridge over the M6 to emerge to cross a lane near Barratt's Farm.

Continue north, diagonally crossing two further fields to reach another lane with Solomon's Temple Farm on the right. Cross the lane, go over the stile opposite and proceed north to go through a mid-hedge gate. Continue to the far right field corner. Go over a stile and walk by the side of the farm lane for about 130 metres. Go left over another stile, the farm drive, and the stile opposite. Continue in a northerly direction over a stile set to the right of High House Farm and then go left along Hardingwood Lane.

Walk the lane for about 400 metres and then go right over a stile and proceed north-west to go over a stile by Parsons Wood. Cross a very long cultivated field aiming for its far left corner, which is near to a stream. Here, cross the lane and proceed up the lane opposite for about 300 metres. Go left along a wooded path. The half-timbered Dove House Farm is clearly visible to the right through the trees.

The path bears right to leave the woods over a stile and to walk the edge of fields before going right over a further stile into bluebell woods. Soon you will emerge to cross two

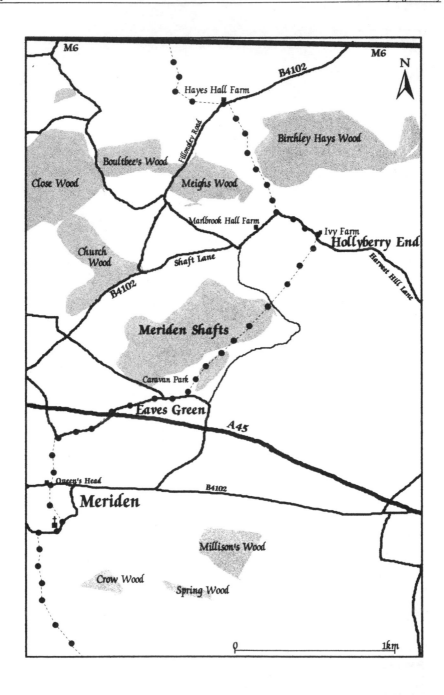

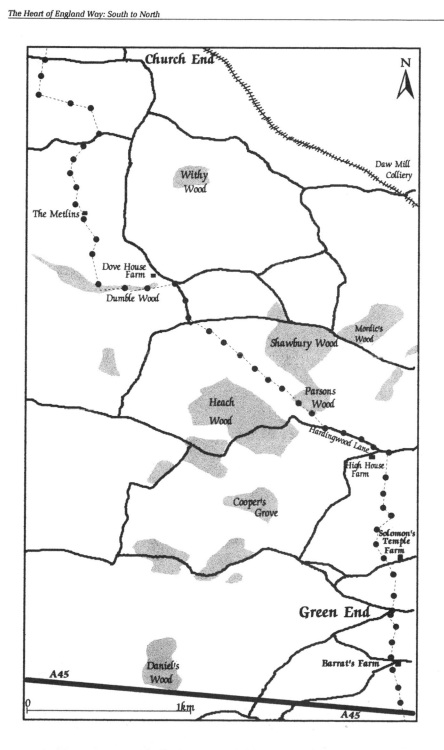

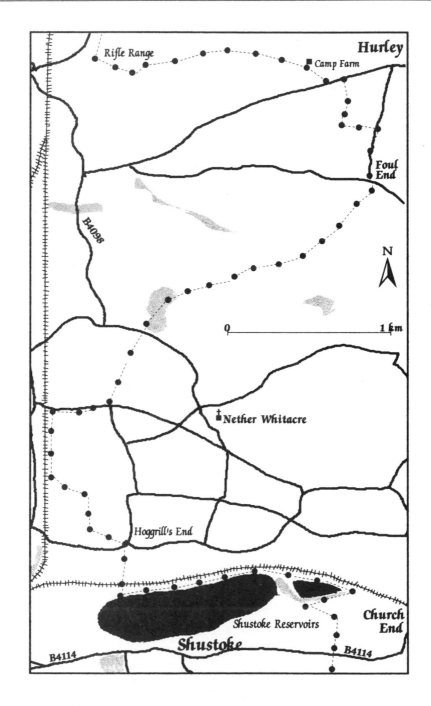

cultivated fields and to reach Metlins House.

Proceed in front of the building then walk by the hedge over several fields and stiles to reach a lane. Go right along the lane. In 100 metres (where the lane bends right), go left over a stile to walk three fields then go left over two stiles to a field corner. Here, go right and proceed over two further stiles to cross the A4114 (Shustoke to Church End) and to descend to the right of a hedge. The waymarked path veers left at a stile then sharp right to lead you by trees near the Shustoke Reservoirs.

In about 350 metres go sharp left to enter the reservoir land over a stile. The path looks as if it should emerge by the reservoir, but sadly the Way walker barely sees the water but goes through a gate to walk by the side of the railway line for over three-quarters of a mile. Just before a railway bridge, go right over a stile to cross the rail track. Go over the stile opposite to ascend a field. In about 300 metres, go over a stile to cross a lane then go through the gate opposite and walk the next field, aiming for yet another stile in the field's opposite corner.

Here, bear right to cross a large field to a pair of stiles. Go left over two footbridges and then right to walk by the side of the railway line for 500 metres – the houses of Whitacre Heath are set on the other side of the track. Go right along a road for about 300 metres and then left over a stile to reach a second stile. Continue north-north-east, ascending two fields to a stile on to a lane. Cross the lane and walk the clear path through woodland. In about 200 metres the path veers north-east through further trees to a gate. Go through the gate and continue on the path. It arcs left over two large fields for more than three-quarters of a mile. The path merges with a track as it arrives at the road in Foul End.

At the road proceed up Dexter Lane opposite. In 400 metres go left along a path by the side of a hedge then right at the field end to go over two stiles before arriving at the road to the west of the village of Hurley. Go left for about 100 metres then go right along the drive to Camp Farm. Pass to the left of the farm buildings and proceed west over a very large cultivated field on a path that curves left towards the buildings and the large wall of the army rifle range.

Proceed, circling to the left of the rifle range, and then cross a road to walk the waymarked path and to go over a stile and a railway line. Proceed along the back of gardens to emerge on the A51 in Kingsbury. Go right up the A51 towards the centre of the town. In about 200 metres go right into Peartree Avenue.

Kingsbury to Weeford

Distance: 9¼ miles (15km)

Duration: 5½ hours

Terrain: Easy walking in typical Warwickshire countryside.

Leave Peartree Avenue car park in Kingsbury and go left to reach the A51. Go right up the road for 100 metres then go left along the road towards Kingsbury Church. Proceed on a path to the right of the church and cross the River Tame footbridge to enter the area of **Kingsbury Water Park**. Continue ahead on an extended footbridge, with the water to your left. Where a thin peninsular of land stretches out into the water, go

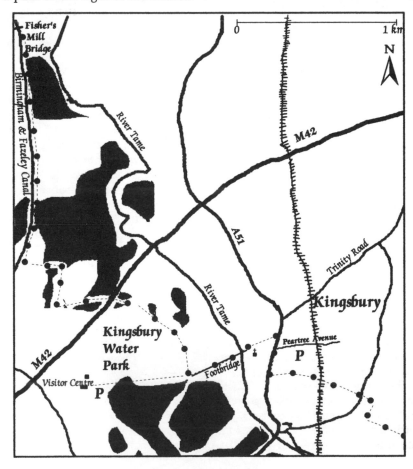

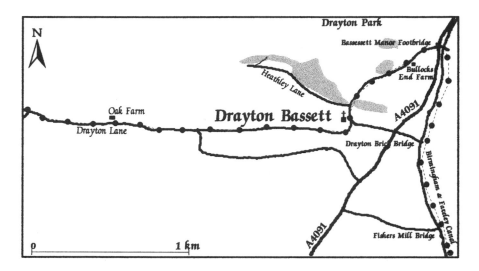

right and walk a tarmac track which curves gently to the left for about 650 metres. Go under the M42 and proceed east through a car park to the right of a camping and caravan site then bear right to emerge near a swivel bridge and the **Birmingham and Fazeley Canal**.

Walk the towpath of the canal and enjoy a very pleasant, easy stretch of peaceful walking, interrupted only by the chugging of the occasional canal boat. In about 2 miles (3.2km) the village of Drayton Bassett will appear to the left. In a further 300 metres you will reach a white, ornate, castellated bridge over the canal.

Cross over the bridge and the A4091 Fazeley to Coleshill road to walk a lane opposite which leads south-west into **Drayton Bassett**. Go past the attractive church and bear right to walk along Drayton Lane for nearly 2 miles (3km) to a T-junction with the A453 Tamworth to Sutton

Coldfield road. Go left by the side of the A453 for about 300 metres and then go right to walk Bangley Lane, passing Great Bangley Farm to arrive by the large farm complex of Hints Farm.

Proceed on a track going left to the front of the farm and then go right through a gate into a large field. Walk the clear track that diagonally crosses the field by a fence, aiming for a stile and ascending past a large oak tree to a further stile in the top left-hand corner of the field. Go over the stile and climb north-west over the next two fields, aiming to the left of Brockhurst Farm to reach a lane.

Go right and walk past the farm, passing Brockhurst Cottages on the right and then the attractive half-timbered Brockhurst Park Farm on the left. About 100 metres beyond this farm, go left between the buildings of Rookery Farm, passing through a gate and walking a fenced farm track by a field. At the field end,

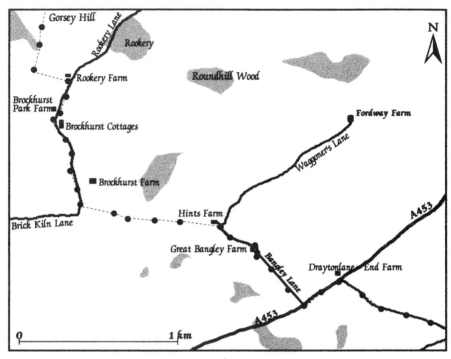

go right over a stile to initially ascend past trees on the left and to go over a further stile. At the brow of the hill proceed north and descend the attractive valley between Gorsey Hill and Rough Leasow, going over a mid-field stile. Continue in a northerly direction to go over another stile and to walk to the left of a hedge. You will go over a further stile and cross Black Brook near the attractive gardens of Bourne House to the left. Go up the lane to reach the A5, going right by the side of the road for about 90 metres before crossing the road. Walk between the buildings of Buck's Head Farm and continue on a clear farm track in a north-east direction for the next mile (1.5km), bearing right then left in front of Buck's Head Cottages. Here, join a green track that descends gently to the right of a hedge over four fields to reach and cross Jerry's Lane.

Weeford to Castle Ring

Distance: 11¼ miles (18km)

Duration: 6 hours

Terrain: Easy walking – initially along a fine track from Packington Moor, later on moorland on the edge of Cannock Chase.

Proceed along the track (near to Packington Moor Farm), going in a north-west direction over a series of fields, going over a number of stiles/gates and passing by Horsley Brook, Ingleyhill and Freehold Home Farms. In just over 1½ miles (2.6km) you will reach and cross the A51 (Lichfield to Tamworth road). Now go left along the pavement towards **Lichfield**.

Go over the bridge over the A38, and in about 650 metres go sharp right up Quarry Hills Lane then immediately left to ascend Hillside to a cul-de-sac. Look for the attractive brass waymarks set in the pavement. By the lamppost go left and walk a fenced footpath which crosses Manor Rise and bears right along Oakhurst to reach and cross over Cherry Orchard. The path continues over the railway line into Station Road, opposite to the Philadelphian Hall. Go left along Station Road, bearing right to cross over the A5127 at a pedestrian crossing and to enter the main shopping centre of the city of Lichfield. Proceed through the shopping area into Dam Street and to the famous cathedral.

Leave the cathedral via The Close, going right along Bird Street then left into Shaw Lane. Go down to the recreation area. Proceed on the clearly waymarked path, going

through a car park and along the back of a row of houses with football pitches and then a golf course to the left.

Continue, going over two stiles to reach the A51 (Stafford – Lichfield road). Cross the busy road with care and go over the stile opposite then walk a field to cross a footbridge. Now aim for and go over a stile in the far corner of the next field and walk a hedged track (with an ancient moat to the right) to reach a lane with Maple Hayes Hall entrance to the left. Go left and walk the lane passing The Abnalls.

In about 500 metres go right over a stile and proceed diagonally north-west over several fields and stiles, climbing to reach Dark Lane by the Keeper's Cottage. Go right along the lane for about 700 metres then go left to leave the lane and to walk by the side of Bilson Brook over a series of fields and stiles.

Cross over Hobstone Hill Lane, walk on to cross Rugeley Road and continue in a westerly direction to enter a lane by a pub. Fifty metres past the pub go right over a stile and continue in a north-west direction by the side of a hedge. Go over a stile in the right-hand corner of the field and veer north to reach a stile to a junction of roads and paths. Here, veer left up a path on Gentleshaw Com-

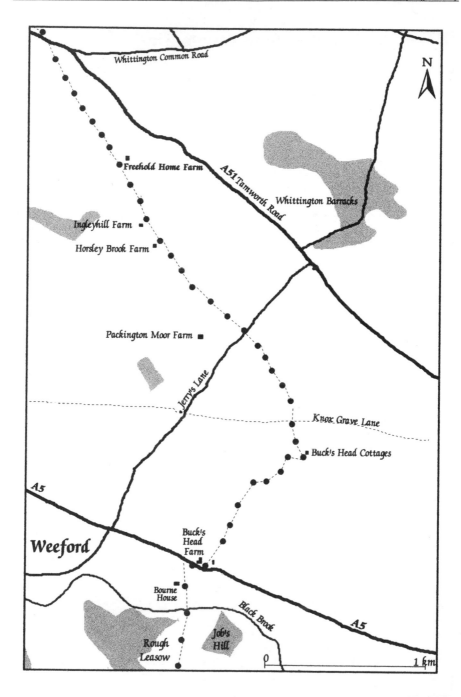

N

Whittington Common Road

A51 Tamworth Road

Whittington Barracks

Freehold Home Farm

Ingleyhill Farm

Horsley Brook Farm

Packington Moor Farm

Jerry's Lane

Knox Grave Lane

Buck's Head Cottages

A5

Weeford

Buck's Head Farm

Bourne House

Black Brook

A5

Rough Leasow

Job's Hill

0   1 km

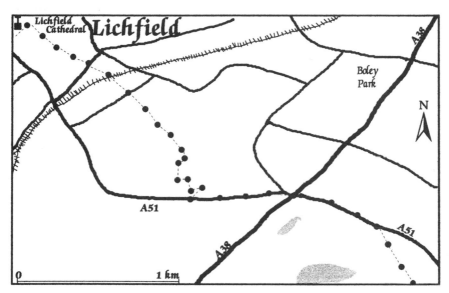

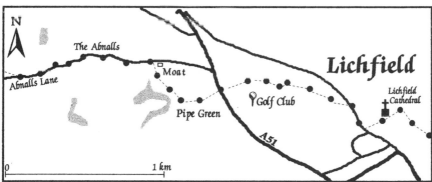

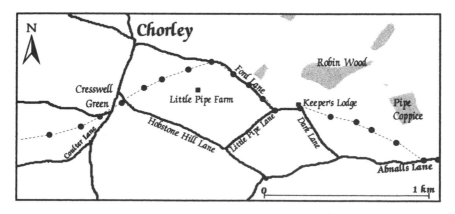

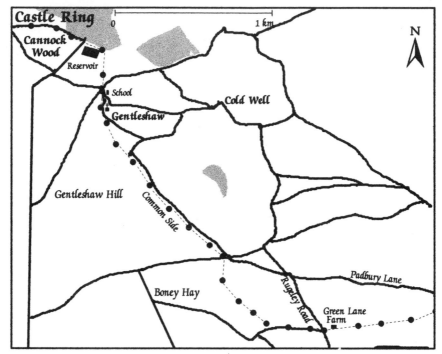

mon with attractive houses to the right (in a north-west direction). Walk this path for about a mile, with the road to your right. The path eventually emerges on the road at the edge of the village of Gentleshaw.

Walk the pavement, passing an attractive brick church and then a school on the right. At the road junction, cross over the road and proceed through a kissing gate along a clear path. At the trees (near the communication mast) go left to walk the edge of woodland and to go through a further kissing gate to a road. Cross the road and walk the pavement of Holly Hill Road for about 500 metres, with houses on the left and the woodland a field away to the right. Go right and enter the car park at **Castle Ring**.

Castle Ring to Milford

Distance: 8¾ miles (14km)

Duration: 5 hours

Terrain: Easy walking over moorland and through delightful woodland on Cannock Chase.

Leave the car park at **Castle Ring** by walking the waymarked path at the rear of the park and proceeding through the trees in a north-west direction to reach a clear track going generally north into **Cannock Chase**. Walk this track for just under a mile (1.5km) through Beaudesert Old Park to approach the Rugeley road. Just before reaching the road go right and continue on a path in a north-east direction for about 300 metres then go left to cross over a junction of four roads. Here, go left on a clearly marked track that becomes Marquis Drive, and then go through two gates before veering left to go past Seven Springs.

Bear right and descend a very attractive valley with a stream and Lower Cliff on the right. Soon you will reach the A460. Cross and then

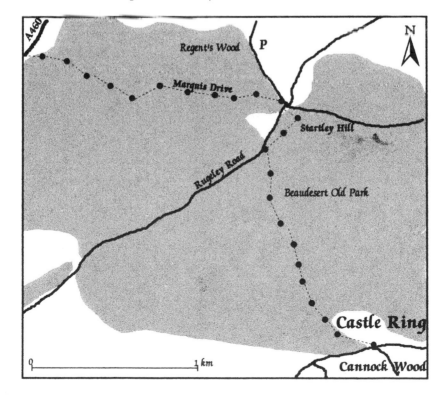

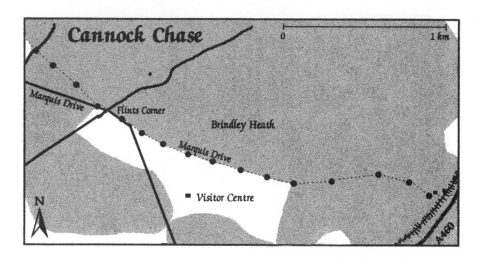

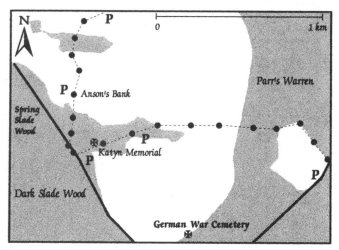

proceed to the left of a railway junction. Cross the rail track and ascend a wide track past a house on your right. The track curves right as it climbs through the trees over Brindley Heath. Walk a stone track to the left of the trees with open land on your left. A Cannock Chase Visitor Centre will soon become visible through some trees on the left – worth a visit.

The Way continues on the track, which has become a tarmac lane. When it reaches a road go right and walk by the roadside to a road junction. Cross the main road (called Penkridge Bank) and continue on a wide path to the right of and veering away from Marquis Drive. In about 600 metres you will cross a further road and then walk to the left of trees to a T-junction of paths.

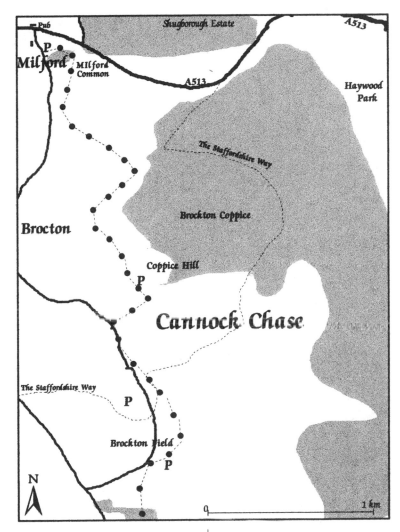

Here, go left and continue on the forestry track, which soon clears the trees for you to enjoy a large open green area. In about 500 metres the track climbs into trees to go through a gate, pass a car park and to reach the Katyn Memorial to some 14,000 Polish soldiers who gave their lives in the Second World War. Proceed along the track to reach a road. Go right and in 25 metres go right again to commence a gentle path ascent to the view point of Anson's Bank.

Continue in a northerly direction to arrive at Chase Road Corner car park. Leave the car park via a path that climbs, curving left and going virtually parallel with the road. In about 600 metres the Staffordshire Way crosses the path of the Heart of England Way. Here, go left and cross a ditch to visit the Glacial Boulder.

Return to the Way, which continues north-west to reach the road. Walk by the side of the road for some 250 metres and then go right to reach a junction of paths. Go left on the second of two tracks and descend gently for about 800 metres. The track bends to the right and then, in about 500 metres, arcs left around a pond. It continues in a north-west direction for about 700 metres to reach a cross-roads of tracks. Go right and then shortly go left to walk the final stretch of the Heart of England Way on a path which descends to the car park in the village of **Milford,** close to **Shugborough Hall.**

Proceed to the road and go right, crossing over to reach the Tourist Office and the end of the Heart of England Way.

20 Circular Walks

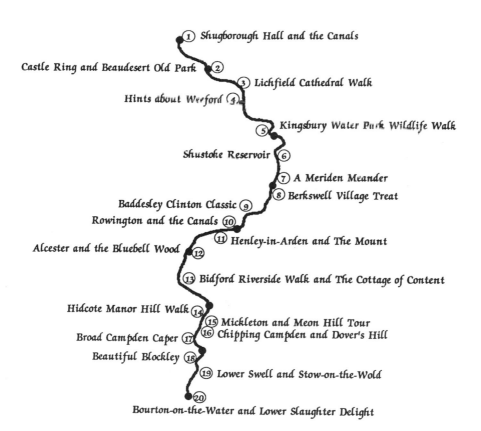

1. Shugborough Hall and the Canals
2. Castle Ring and Beaudesert Old Park
3. Lichfield Cathedral Walk
4. Hints about Weeford
5. Kingsbury Water Park Wildlife Walk
6. Shustoke Reservoir
7. A Meriden Meander
8. Berkswell Village Treat
9. Baddesley Clinton Classic
10. Rowington and the Canals
11. Henley-in-Arden and The Mount
12. Alcester and the Bluebell Wood
13. Bidford Riverside Walk and The Cottage of Content
14. Hidcote Manor Hill Walk
15. Mickleton and Meon Hill Tour
16. Chipping Campden and Dover's Hill
17. Broad Campden Caper
18. Beautiful Blockley
19. Lower Swell and Stow-on-the-Wold
20. Bourton-on-the-Water and Lower Slaughter Delight

Walk 1: Shugborough Hall and the Canals

Starting from Milford Common, this fine walk climbs to pass Shugborough Hall, crosses the River Trent over a superb packhorse bridge then joins the towpath of the Trent and Mersey Canal. It meets the Staffordshire and Worcestershire Canal for an easy towpath walk past colourful narrow boats on the return to Milford Common

Distance: 4 miles (6km); **Duration:** 2 to 2½ hours

Car Parking: Free car park at Milford, on the Common (SJ 973211)

Refreshments: The Barley Mow pub, situated on the road junction at Milford Common, is a large, attractive, rambling inn with Victorian-style décor. It is a regular watering hole for visitors to Shugborough Hall and walkers of Cannock Chase.

Map: OS Explorer 6 Cannock Chase and Chasewater

Terrain: One steep ascent but otherwise easy walking

Place names: throughout the route descriptions, wherever a place name appears in bold within the walks, you will find a detailed description of the place in the final section of this book.

From the car park, proceed north-east towards the main entrance gates of **Shugborough Hall**. At the A513, go right and walk past the main entrance to the hall, with its pair of fine **Milford** Lodges (1800). Continue along the side of the wall. At the wall end, go left and climb a steep path that runs to the right of the park wall – a very pleasant stretch of countryside walking after the initial short hill. At the hilltop, proceed past a raised reservoir (enclosed in railings) and walk the path ahead (do not take the path to the left) going generally east through attractive trees and ferns. Descend through Stafford Plantation and you will soon reach the A513 once again. Go left along the footpath, passing by

the entrance to Shugborough Working Farm Museum. After about 350 metres, go left over a stile to a path and join the driveway to the Farm Museum. Here, pass to the right of the museum complex then proceed ahead by walking a fenced tarmac track, from where you will enjoy a fine view of the magnificent Shugborough Hall to your left.

Continue along the track/lane, passing by the tradesman's entrance to the hall and going over Essex Bridge. This splendid 16th-century packhorse bridge over the River Trent has 14 fine arches and is just 1.2 metres (4ft) wide. After crossing the river bridge, continue up the lane. Just before bridge number 73 of the Trent and Mersey Canal, go right and descend through a hand gate to the canal towpath. Go left under the bridge to walk past Haywood Lock, where you will normally see a large number of narrow boats and small motor boats moored.

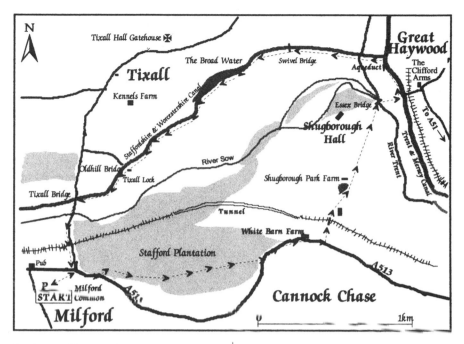

At Great Haywood Junction go left under an elegant, sweeping arch bridge to join the towpath of the Staffordshire and Worcestershire Canal. It is here that the Staffordshire and Worcestershire Canal crosses the River Trent on an aqueduct to join the Trent and Mersey Canal. Boat repair facilities are available and narrow boats tend to congregate along this stretch of canal. Proceed along the towpath of the Staffs. and Worcs. Canal, passing the colourful narrow boats as you walk beneath a swivel bridge (No. 108) to reach Tixall Wide – a 300-metre stretch of the canal which was deliberately widened to form a sort of lake to the former Tixall Hall. Up to the right one can see a structure which appears like a folly. It is, in fact, the massive 16th-century gatehouse

(one of the largest in the country) to the former Tixall Hall. It is three storeys high, richly decorated with Roman, Ionic and Corinthian columns, and has four impressive, tall turrets. People fishing from the narrow boats make an interesting scene as you walk past Tixall Wide.

As you proceed along the towpath you will pass beneath Oldhill Bridge (No. 107) and soon reach Tixall Lock. You will exit the towpath at bridge number 106. Go over Tixall Bridge then walk on the roadside over the River Sow and over a railway bridge. There follows a short pavement ascent to **Milford** Common. Cross over the A513 and return to the car park.

Walk 2: Castle Ring and Beaudesert Old Park

Get away from the buzz of modern life with this pleasant stroll through Beaudesert Old Park on Cannock Chase. This former home of the Pagets (Marquises of Anglesey) was once a huge deer park for royalty and the nobility, but is now delightful woodland and heathland for all to enjoy.

Distance: 5 miles (8km); **Duration:** 3 hours

Car Parking: Free car park at Castle Ring

Refreshments: The Park Gate Inn dates to about 1640 and was originally part of the Marquis of Anglesey's estate and the venue for stately banquets. Today, being positioned almost opposite to the Castle Ring car park, it provides welcome refreshment to walkers.

Map: OS Outdoor Leisure 6 Cannock Chase and Chasewater

Terrain: Undulating

Leave the car park at **Castle Ring** by walking the waymarked (Heart of England Way) path at the rear of the park and proceeding through the trees in a north-west direction to reach a clear, broad, green track going generally north into **Cannock Chase**. Walk this track for just under a mile (1.5km) through Beaudesert Old Park. Initially you will descend as you proceed ahead at a junction of paths and then bear left at the fork to cross over a small stream by an attractive forest pool. There follows an uphill stretch that leads north towards the Rugeley road.

Just before reaching the road, go right and continue on a path in a north-easterly direction for about 300 metres then go left to cross over Rugeley Road at a junction of four roads. Here, go left on a clearly marked track that becomes Marquis Drive, and then go through two gates before veering left to go past Seven Springs. This delightful track bears right and descends a very attractive

valley with a stream and Lower Cliff on the right – keep an eye open for kingfishers as you descend by the stream towards a road.

Just before reaching the road, go sharp left to pass a forestry barrier and climb a track bearing generally south through the trees. Bear right at a fork in the track and then proceed ahead at a junction of paths/tracks. The track ascends between impressive conifers then levels before you reach a crossroads of tracks. You will soon reach the perimeter of a golf course. Proceed along the path over the golf course, taking appropriate care not to interfere with the golfing world, until you reach a further junction of tracks. At this crossroads, continue ahead and you will descend to the Rugeley road once again.

Go left along the road for about 200 metres then, when opposite to the car park entrance to the golf club, go right past a forestry barrier and continue by walking a conifer-lined

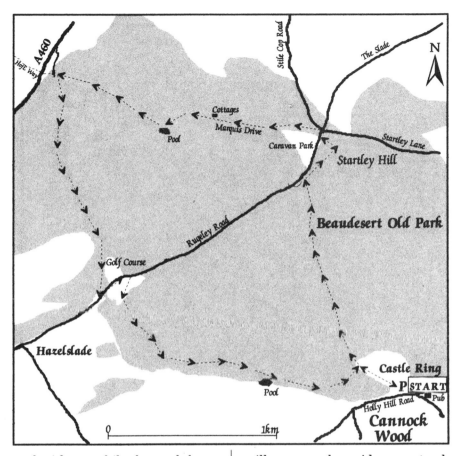

track. After a while the track bears
left (to a south-east direction) to pass
by a large pool (once a colliery pit!).
The track now gently climbs through
the forest to a crossroads of tracks.
Here, bear left (north-east) and you
will soon reach a wide green track.
Cross the track and ascend the path
to the left and opposite into the trees.
In about 70 metres go right and walk
the path back to the **Castle Ring** car
park.

Walk 3: Lichfield Cathedral Walk

A visit to the beautiful city of Lichfield to see its unique three-spired medieval cathedral, plus a meander through the attractive local countryside

Distance: 4½ miles (7km); **Duration:** 3 hours

Car Parking: Pay and Display car park in Pool Walk near to Minster Pool (SK 116097)

Refreshments: There are numerous eating/drinking establishments in the city of Lichfield, or you may prefer The George and Dragon, The Feathers or The Fountain in Beacon Street.

Maps: OS Explorer 6 Cannock Chase and Chasewater, Pathfinder 872 Rugeley and Lichfield (North)

Terrain: Mostly on the level

From the car park, aim towards the Minster Pool, bearing right into Dam Street to join the Heart of England Way. Now go left and the magnificent **Lichfield Cathedral** will be ahead of you. Bear left to reach the front of the cathedral – which you should spare time to visit while your boots are clean. When you are ready, leave the cathedral via The Close, going right along Bird Street then left into Shaw Lane and descend to reach the recreation area. Proceed on the clearly waymarked path going through a car park and along the back of a row of houses, with football pitches and then a golf course to the left.

Continue, going over two stiles to reach the A51 (Stafford to Lichfield road). Cross the busy road with care and go over the stile opposite then walk a field to cross a footbridge. Now aim for and go over a stile in the far corner of the next field and walk a hedged track (with an ancient moat to the right) to reach Abnalls Lane. Maple Hayes Hall (a dyslexia school)

is to the left. Go right along the lane for about 120 metres, then go left over a stile at a public footpath sign and walk to the right of the hedge of a cultivated field. You will cross to the left side of the hedge before going over a further stile into Cross in Hand Lane.

Go left and ascend the narrow lane for 250 metres then, just after the entrance drive to Lyncroft Cottage, go right and walk a pleasant hedged path which proceeds north to arrive at the A51 (Stafford to Lichfield road). Cross the A51 and go right along a footpath that is set in trees above the road level. Walk to a road junction with traffic lights. Here, go left along the pavement of Eastern Avenue (the A5192). Proceed past the entrance to Friars Grange Sports Centre and you will soon reach Grange Lane. Cross over the lane and veer left up some steps and onto a path in a (mainly) conifer plantation. Continue north-east along the clear path which meanders through the trees with glimpses of

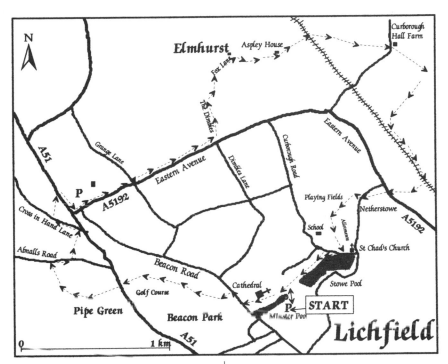

Lichfield to the right and pastureland to the left. In about 500 metres the path reaches the open, with Dimbles Lane on the other side of Eastern Avenue. You will see some steps up from Eastern Avenue. Here, go left onto a driveway and continue north-east to cross over the entrance drive to a car parking area.

Proceed on the clear path opposite (known as The Dimbles), initially descending between trees to go over Circuit Brook and then climbing between ivy-clad trees to reach a green lane (Fox Lane) which leads into the pleasant hamlet of Elmhurst. At the end of the green lane, go right onto a farm track that arcs left to pass a finger-post as you join the Darwin Way, going north-east. Walk this

clear track past Apsley House and then, where the track (now a concrete lane) bends sharp right, proceed ahead over a field, heading towards a railway line. Go over the stile to the railway and cross the line (the trains speed through so take care). Proceed over the stile opposite and continue in a south-east direction over several fields – you will go through a kissing gate, by the side of an electric pylon and through a farm gate to arrive on a lane by Curborough Hall Farm complex.

Walk past a small antique centre and go to the right of the farm buildings, a number of which now house an art and craft industry. At the sign to Field House, walk to the right of the drive's hedge. Bear left at its bend to go over a footbridge and stile in the top left-hand corner of the field. Here you will leave the Darwin Way and go right (south-west) to walk by the side of a babbling, small brook. Reach and go over a stile in the field corner so that you can continue on your path line with the three spires of Lichfield Cathedral now prominent ahead on the skyline. The path bears left to go over a stile then runs generally parallel with the railway line to your right. Continue over several stiles with a farm lane to your left until you reach a bridge over the railway. Cross over the bridge and proceed over Chadswell Heights road into a dead-end residential lane. Immediately after the first house, go left and walk a tarmac footpath behind houses. You will soon emerge in Spring Road. Now walk ahead and go right at the road corner along a further footpath, which leads into Netherstowe Lane. Here, go right to cross over Eastern Avenue and to walk the footpath opposite into Verdi Court and then to reach Netherstowe Road.

Cross the road and walk Handel Walk – to the right and opposite. This path leads to a footpath/cycleway in pleasant parkland. Bear left and walk this path, initially to the left of football pitches and later past allotments, until you reach St Chad's Road. You will see the impressive St Chad's Church to your left as you cross the road and go up steps to a walkway and a fine view of Stowe Pool. Bear right and walk the poolside path. Fishermen, ducks, coots, moorhens and seagulls add to a pleasant view.

At the end of the pool you will cross over Bishop's Walk to arrive in Reeve Lane. This leads you back into Dam Street, near that most impressive cathedral. If you go left over the bridge you will enjoy a delightful view of Minster Pool on your return to the car park.

Lichfield cathedral

Walk 4: Hints about Weeford

The walk includes a delightful descent of Rough Leasow followed by a pleasant woodland meander back to the hamlet of Hints.

Distance: 4 miles (km); **Duration:** 2 to 2½ hours

Car Parking: Park on the grass verge in Rookery Lane, near to the village hall in the hamlet of Hints (SK 157031).

Refreshments: There are no pubs along the route of the path, but about 1¼ miles west of Weeford, The Hollybush at Little Hay will be pleased to welcome a thirsty rambler.

Map: OS Pathfinder 892 Lichfield and Brownhills

Terrain: Easy walking through attractive Warwickshire countryside but with a couple of undulations.

From the village hall in Hints, descend Rookery Lane towards a ford over Black Brook. About 50 metres before the ford go left to join a footpath through the trees which leads to a church gate. As you go through the gate you will be impressed by the fine church building, but continue to the gate beyond which leads to the main road through the village.

Go right and descend this peaceful road, passing by Botley House on the left. Where the road ends, go right through trees and over a couple of stiles to walk a clear path climbing south by a field hedge. Aim for a further stile in the top left-hand corner of the field. Go over the stile and into Roundhill Wood (in spring you will be able to admire the beautiful rhododendrons which seem to be everywhere). The path veers left into a wood-side field. Continue south by the side of the wood then descend by the side of the hedge to an electric pylon.

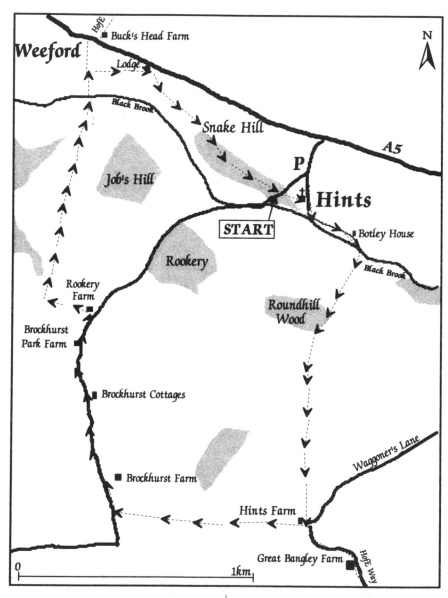

Pass to the left of the pylon and now continue in a southerly direction, aiming for three oak trees set towards the top left-hand part of the large cultivated field. As you cross a track you will see a small finger-post which will direct you south to a hedge stile. Hints Farm appears in the distance. Proceed over pastureland, aiming to the immediate left of the farm complex, and go through a gate on to Waggoner's Lane – here you go right to join the Heart of England Way.

Proceed on a track going in the front of the farm and then go right through a gate into a large field. Walk the clear track that diagonally crosses the field by a fence, aiming for a stile. Go up past a large oak tree to a further stile in the top left-hand corner of the field. Go over the stile and ascend west-north-west over the next field, aiming to the left of Brockhurst Farm. Here you will reach a lane.

At the lane, go right and walk past the farm. Continue, passing by Brockhurst Cottages on the right and then the attractive, half-timbered Brockhurst Park Farm on the left. About 100 metres beyond this farm, go left between the buildings of Rookery Farm. Pass through a gate and walk a fenced farm track by a field. At the field end, go right over a stile. Initially, climb past trees on the left, and then go over a further stile. At the brow of the hill proceed north and descend the most attractive valley between Gorsey Hill and Rough Leasow, going over a mid-field stile. Continue heading north to go over another stile and to walk to the left of a hedge. You will go over a further stile and cross Black Brook near the attractive gardens of Bourne House to the left.

About 130 metres after crossing over Black Brook, go right through a kissing gate to walk a field path to the left of low metal railings. There are fine views of Rough Leasow and Gorsey Hill to your right. In 300 metres go over the stile in the field corner, with The Lodge to your left. Now go right and walk a clear, wide green path below Snake's Hill, initially to the left of a fence and then crossing open land towards a farm gate at the entrance to woodland.

Proceed along the farm track through this woodland of silver birch trees. This delightful stretch of walking ends all too soon when you reach Rookery Lane, with your car parked up to the left.

Walk 5: Kingsbury Water Park Wildlife Walk

A very pleasant, easy stroll around the delightful Kingsbury Water Park and an opportunity to see many birds.

Distance: 3½ miles (km); **Duration:** 2 to 2½ hours

Car Parking: Free parking in Pear Tree Avenue, Kingsbury (SP 218963)

Refreshments: There are a number of pubs in Kingsbury that will be pleased to serve the thirsty walker.

Map: OS Pathfinder 914 Nuneaton

Terrain: Easy

From the car park, go left along Pear Tree Avenue to reach and cross the A51 with care. Turn right and walk up the pavement for about 120 metres. Go left to walk by the churchyard and then proceed towards the River Tame, descending steps to reach the entrance footbridge to

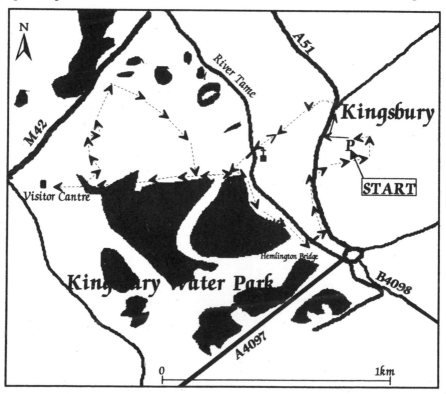

Kingsbury Water Park. Cross the bridge over the Tame and walk the long, raised footpath until you reach a narrow land stretch to the left. Here, proceed ahead, going generally west to reach the Visitor Centre.

When you are ready to move on, retrace your steps to the end of the parking area and go left on a wide, stone footpath going north. In about 700 metres you will reach a junction of paths. The busy M42 is to your left. Now go right and walk the easy bridleway past Kingsbury Pool and the Far Leys complex. The Heart of England bridleway arcs gently to the

right, and in about 650 metres you will arrive back at the long, raised footbridge. Return along the footbridge/footpath but just before you reach the bridge over the River Tame, go right on a clear path with the river on your left and Hemlingford Water on your right.

Where the path divides, keep to the left path (the right one merely follows the bank of Hemlingford Water) and in about 200 metres you will reach a cycleway lane. Now go left along the lane to cross over Hemlington Bridge. Just before the sign 'Kingsbury Road', go left over a stile into riverside pastureland and walk the clear path to the left of the road hedge. As you near the field end, go over the stile to the right and on to the pavement of Kingsbury's Coventry road (A51).

Go left and when you reach Church Lane, cross the A51 with care and enter the common land opposite on a path which proceeds ahead to the south of the gardens. In about 200 metres, go left to ascend Wright Close and to reach Pear Tree Avenue. Go left and in 75 metres you will reach the car park and your car.

Walk 6: Shustoke Reservoir

A delightful walk around the boats on Shustoke Reservoir.

Distance: 3½ miles (6km); **Duration:** 2 hours

Car Parking: In the car park of the Griffin Inn with permission of the landlord (SP 242909), or in the car park of Shustoke Reservoir (SP 225910).

Refreshments: The Griffin Inn, a 200-year-old brick building, was originally an ale house and the landlord used to a make coffins in the adjacent barn. Today the pub is famous for its micro-brewery, which produces enticing local beers such as Gravedigger's Ale – it is a popular watering hole for local ramblers who enjoy the in-house ale.

Map: OS Pathfinder 914 Nuneaton

Terrain: Easy

Start from the Griffin Inn and proceed up Shawbury Lane into the village of Church End. After about 50 metres, go right (opposite the lane to St Cuthbert's Church) over a stile into pastureland. Continue over two fields and go right at the hedge of the second field to join the Heart of England Way.

Proceed east over two further fields, going over a stile to reach the corner of the second field where you go right. Continue north over two further stiles to reach Church Road (Shustoke to Church End). Cross the road and go over the stile opposite, descending to the right of a hedge. The waymarked path veers left at a stile, bearing north-west to the bottom of the field. You then go left again and walk a clear path going generally south-west. You will go over a stile and then walk to the left of the hedge of a private lane. There

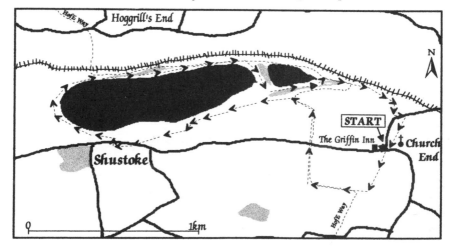

is a fine view of the picturesque reservoir over the hedge until you drop
down to join the lane (Bixhill Lane).
The local sailing club uses this part
of the reservoir and it can be a colourful place during summer months.
Walk the lane for about 600 metres,
passing by houses and bungalows
until you reach the B4114 in the village of Shustoke.

Go right along the pavement for
some 200 metres then go right again
to arrive at a Severn Trent's car park.
As you follow the road towards the
parking area you will go past the
public toilets and will then see a finger-post indicating a circular path
which will take you round on the
bank above the reservoir. Follow the
route – it initially circles clockwise
around the larger of the two reservoirs, where sailing boats can be
seen. This is a delightful walk that arrives at steps leading to a central
strip of land. Go right and across the
land, going south – from here you

can enjoy fine views in either direction. At the end of the land strip bear
left to continue on the circular walk.
It is set a small distance to the south
of the smaller reservoir to protect
you from possible danger of fly fishing lines. After passing behind the
buildings of the fly fishermen's club,
leave the reservoir complex over a
stile and continue ahead to the right
of the railway line.

The clear path will take you
through woodland to emerge via a
stile to walk the bottom of a large
field. Circle the edge of the field,
climbing to the B4114 by the entrance to Watson Petroleum Depot.
Go left along the road edge for about
75 metres then cross over to go
through a kissing gate into
pastureland below St Cuthbert's
Church. Go up the field and through
a second kissing gate set to the right
of the churchyard. Walk a lane past
the church up to Shawbury Lane. At
the lane, go right to reach a road corner of the B4114 – the Griffin Inn is
opposite.

Walk 7: A Meriden Meander

A pleasant woodland walk around the very centre of England.

Distance: 4½ miles (7km); **Duration:** 2½ to 3 hours

Car Parking: Park by the roadside opposite The Queen's Head (SP 252821)

Refreshments: The Queen's Head pub, set in a convenient position between walking days on the Heart of England Way, is a regular eating place for walkers.

Map: OS Pathfinder 935 Coventry (North) and Meriden

Terrain: fairly flat

From the Queen's Head pub in Meriden, proceed up Walsh Lane and in about 300 metres go right (with Village Farm on your left) to walk a narrow lane. In 400 metres it dips beneath the main A45 Birmingham to Coventry road. Continue along the lane into Eaves Green.

In the village you will pass by a caravan park and then go left over a stile to a track which leads through the fine woodland of Meriden Shafts. Proceed over a second stile then walk over two further fields and enter trees over a further stile. Walk the lovely path through the woods and go over a stile at its end. Now go left and continue along the clear bridleway, leaving the Heart of England Way as it goes right into pastureland. This is a beautiful track that soon is hedged with attractive holly bushes (covered with red berries in the winter). Near to Stonehouse Farm the track becomes a lane, and in about 400 metres you will reach a road junction. Here, bear left and then right to walk Beck's Lane, going in a generally north-west direction. In about 250 metres the lane bends right near the entrance to Beck's Farm. Here, go over the stile to

the right of the farm drive then proceed on a waymarked path over a field and through a couple of small gates to reach a road.

Cross the road to the stile opposite. Proceed over the field to a further stile on to a quiet lane near to two large communication masts. Continue ahead along the lane for about 300 metres – ahead you will see a further communication mast. Go left through a hedge gap 50 metres before the mast and walk a clear path set to the left of Close Wood. You will enter the wood via a further stile and can then enjoy a delightful stretch of woodland walking.

Exit Close Wood and walk the clear path over cultivated land to reach High Ash Farm and a farm track/lane. Go left and descend the track/lane in a south-easterly direction. Go over the stile by the locked gate and bear right to descend a lane going past Lodge Green Farm to reach Fillongley Road. Cross the main road and continue down Lodge Green Lane opposite for about 350 metres. Now go right over a stile to walk open land on a clear path that follows a line of oak trees – a pleasant stretch of walking which soon ends

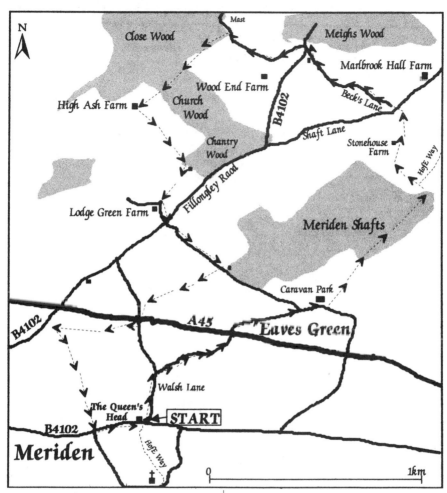

as you near the noisy A45. At the end of the large field go left along the lane to cross the A45. At the end of the bridge, go right over a stile to walk a diversion path high above the A45.

In 100 metres go left over a stile into pastureland and aim for a footbridge set to the right of a pond surrounded by trees. From the footbridge, walk up the next field, going east to a pair of field corner stiles. Now bear sharp left over the second stile to descend over several fields in a south-easterly direction. As you descend and approach the town of Meriden, the view of the hilltop church impresses. Aim to the left of a row of newish bungalows and go over a stile to the access road to The Queen's Head. Go left and walk back to your car.

Walk 8: Berkswell Village Treat

A delightful walk around the estates of Berkswell Hall. The final part of the walk is through the park, passing by its attractive lake.

Distance: 3½ miles (6km); **Duration:** 2 hours

Car Parking: Park in the car park of The Bear Inn (SP 247791) with permission, or in the lay-by on the Meriden road (SP 246793).

Refreshments: The Bear Inn is a fine, 16th-century timbered pub and often described as 'the perfect example of an old English inn'. It was once part of the Berkswell estate, and in 1874 was called the Bear and Ragged Staff. It is believed to have had links with the Civil War and a helmet, a boot and two 1707 coins have been found. Today it is a very attractive pub where walkers will receive a warm welcome.

Maps: OS Pathfinders 935 Coventry (North) and Meriden, and 955 Coventry (South) and Kenilworth

Terrain: Easy walking, generally flat

From The Bear Inn, descend the road opposite into **Berkswell**, sparing time to enjoy the beautiful village. Just before the gateway to the church, go right through a kissing gate and walk the path by the side of the churchyard. Exit the path via a gate, descending via a stile and fur-

ther kissing gate to the Meriden road. Go left and walk the footpath going past the turn off of the Heart of England Way. About 150 metres beyond the entrance to Home Farm, cross the road and go left into a driveway just past Wilmot Cottage and through a gate into pastureland. The path pro-

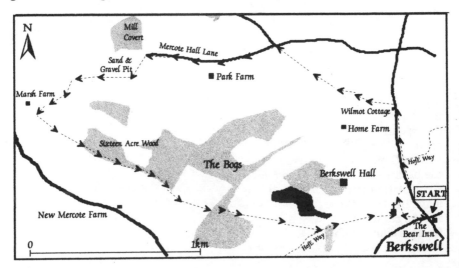

ceeds to the right of a hedge, going over a couple of stiles and with a clear view of the large complex of Home Farm to your left. Now diagonally climb a very large cultivated field on a clear path heading in a north-easterly direction. In about 500 metres you will reach a lane corner via a stile.

Go left and walk Mercote Hall Lane for about 750 metres, going east and passing Park Farm – this is a very quiet farm lane and you are unlikely to meet any traffic. Continue along the lane, passing around a large fenced sand and gravel pit. At the end of the enclosed area, go left over footbridges then climb to the left of a hedge towards Marsh Farm.

Just beyond the farm, go left and walk by the hedge towards Sixteen Acre Wood. Enter the wood over a stile and walk the beautiful track at the wood's edge for 650 metres – this is a delightful stretch of woodland walking, particularly in the autumn when the ground is covered with golden leaves. Continue by the hedge to enter a strip of trees, then leave the trees via a stile to commence a fine parkland walk. Walk the clear path

going east-south-east and you will admire the magnificent view of Berkswell Hall Lake ahead. This delightful view can be enjoyed for some 600 metres, when you will enter trees and go through a kissing gate to rejoin the Heart of England Way. Cross the track and proceed over a stile to a planked area with the hall to your left. Continue through a gate and then a kissing gate to arrive near the superb church in **Berkswell** – worth a photograph. Continue along the road, bearing left to reach a road junction, and The Bear Inn will be on your right.

An English Ash – typical of the fine trees to be seen

Walk 9: Baddesley Clinton Classic

A delightful stroll along the side of the Grand Union Canal, passing through attractive Warwickshire countryside. There is also an opportunity to visit the beautiful Baddesley Clinton Manor (NT).

Distance: 4½ miles (7km); **Duration:** 2½ to 3 hours

Car Parking: The Navigation Inn (SP 191279)

Refreshments: The Navigation Inn is a pleasant canal-side pub which welcomes walkers.

Maps: OS Pathfinders 954 Solihull and Alvechurch, and 955 Coventry (South) and Kenilworth

Terrain: Generally flat and easy walking

From the Navigation Inn car park, go right to cross over the Kingswood Bridge (No. 65) over the Grand Union Canal, cross the road and descend to the towpath of the canal. Go left under the bridge and walk the canal-side footpath, going north for about 1½ miles (2.5km). If you start the walk in the morning you will enjoy superb canal reflections. Pass beneath Rising Bridge (No. 66) and a fine pipe bridge before passing a well-maintained farm complex as you leave the canal at Turnover Bridge (No. 67).

Cross over Turnover Bridge and proceed east over a stile into pastureland. Then go over a smart, gated footbridge and walk to the right of a field hedge until you veer right to a hedged farm track. Leave the track via a stile at a junction of lanes, which you cross and continue south-east along Netherwood Lane opposite. In about 200 metres, just before the first (large) house on the right, go right over a stile and walk a hedged/fenced path going generally south. Go over two more stiles then left to walk by the field hedge until you reach a wide, green bridle path.

Go left (south-east) along this track for 350 metres, negotiating a couple of stiles then bearing right to join the Heart of England Way by the gates to Convent Farm. Walk the drive of the converted convent to reach Rising Lane on the edge of the village of **Baddesley Clinton**. Go right at the lane. At the next lane corner bear left at a road sign 'Mousley End 2, Hay Wood 1' and walk past the very modern Manor Park Farm. In 300 metres, just before the main entrance to Bromes Park, go right over stiles and continue on the Heart of England Way on a hedged path. This circles the park perimeter, passing in and out of attractive woodland before reaching the entrance drive (NT) to Baddesley Clinton Manor via a small kissing gate.

Do spare time to visit the beautiful manor, its fine gardens and also the attractive village church. Otherwise, cross the entrance drive and leave the Heart of England Way over the stile opposite to enter the parkland of the manor. The impressive moated building offers an intriguing vista to your left as you continue to the right of trees. Through the trees

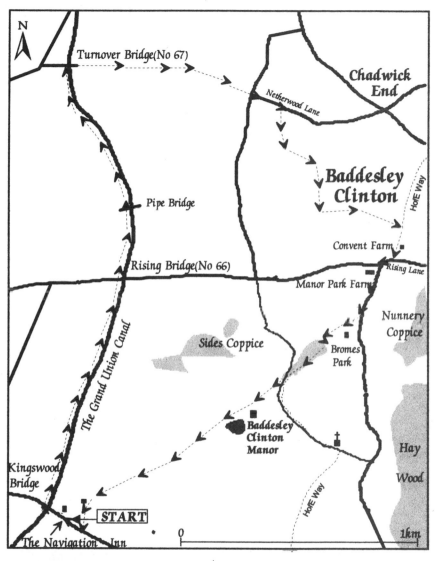

you will get glimpses of the gardens and maybe the small lake. After going over a stile at the bottom of the trees, the path proceeds south-east by a field hedge, with pleasant views over Kingswood to the right. At the field stile aim to the left of a red-brick

farm workshop and proceed beneath the electricity wires. Go over a stile and walk through the farm complex and along the farm drive to arrive at the B4439. Go right and in 100 metres you will arrive at the car park of The Navigation Inn.

Walk 10: Rowington and the Canals

A walk through typical Warwickshire countryside and along the towpaths of two of the most attractive canals in the Midlands. The set of nine Lapworth Locks is a sight to behold.

Distance: 7 miles (11km); **Duration:** 3½ to 4 hours

Car Parking: Tom o' the Wood Inn, Finwood Road, Rowington (SP 193696) or the canal-side car park at Kingswood Brook (SP 186711)

Refreshments: Tom o' the Wood Inn, named after a local windmill some 25 years ago, was originally called the New Inn. Today it is popular with walkers and canal users alike.

Maps: OS Pathfinders 954 Solihull and Alvechurch, and 975 Redditch and Henley-in-Arden

Terrain: Easy walking on the level

Leave the Tom o' the Wood Inn car park, going left to cross over Turner's Green Bridge then left again to descend to the towpath of the Grand Union Canal. Go under the bridge and proceed north along the attractive towpath for a little under three-quarters of a mile (1.1km). You will pass beneath Weston Hall Bridge (No. 64), then soon go left along the towpath of a link canal between the Grand Union and the Stratford-on-Avon Canals, passing beneath the railway bridge to reach the Kingswood Junction of the Stratford-on-Avon Canal. Here, bear right to continue on the left bank of the Stratford-on-Avon Canal, going north to reach a flight of nine lock gates at Lapworth.

When you have reached the top lock gate (No. 9), turn around and descend by the side of these amazing gates. Each gate is spaced only a few metres from its neighbour and the afternoon view in the summer is a colourful spectacle of narrow boats

working their way through the sequence of locks. Between each of these nine lock gates there is a larger reservoir of water to permit the manoeuvring of the long narrow boats and they provide a sort of isthmus. Continue south, passing by Kingswood Junction, and cross the Stratford-on-Avon Canal to walk the towpath, now on the left bank. Pause at Dick Lane Bridge, an old, cast-iron split bridge that was built in two halves and designed with a gap for the towing rope used on the original horse-drawn boats. After a further 1¼ miles (1.9km) of delightful walking you will arrive at a very narrow lock gate by the Finwood Bridge (No. 40). It can be very entertaining to watch narrow boats progress through this particular lock. Go left over the stile by the bridge and onto the road (Mill Lane).

Go left and walk up Mill Lane for nearly a mile (1.5km) as it passes through the village of Finwood and goes over the M40. On the other side

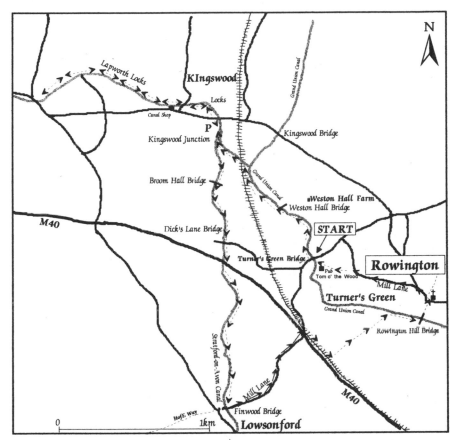

of the bridge over the M40, go right and walk a lane cutting that runs parallel with the motorway for some 300 metres. At the brow of the cutting go left and walk the pleasant track that in about 400 metres bends right to go by the side of and above the Grand Union Canal. At Rowington Hill Bridge (No. 62) go left to cross the canal and to ascend a rural lane to reach the old Warwick road in Rowington. The village church will be facing you.

Go left and walk the pavement of the B4439 through Rowington. In just over 100 metres, bear left to walk down Mill Lane and to stroll past attractive private residences for some 400 metres. Now bear left and walk Badger Lane. Just before the entrance to Field Cottage, go left over a stile and enjoy the pleasant view of colourful narrow boats on the Grand Union Canal below. Descend by the field hedge to the right and go over a stile at its corner. Take care as you will pass through the grounds of a small farmhouse to reach a final stile to the road outside the Tom o' the Wood Inn car park.

Walk 11: Henley-in-Arden and The Mount

After an initial hill ascent to enjoy the superb views from the top of Beaudesert Mount this walk takes you through gently rolling Warwickshire countryside. A descent to stroll the towpath of the Stratford-upon-Avon Canal leads to a meander along the banks of the River Alne as you return to the historic Tudor town of Henley-in-Arden.

Distance: 5 miles (8km); **Duration:** 3 hours

Car Parking: Park by the roadside in Beaudesert Lane, Henley-in-Arden (SP 153659)

Refreshments: The White Swan Hotel, High Street, Henley-in-Arden was built about 450 years ago to replace an earlier inn which dated from 1352. It became a popular coaching inn in the mid-19th century, being set on a Birmingham to London route, and then until 1903 was the home of the local court. Samuel Johnson stayed at the inn and is believed to have written one of his books here. One of the upstairs rooms is said to be haunted by an 18-year-old girl, Virginia Black, who died in the inn after falling down the staircase after a row with her lover. Today the inn is a regular watering hole for local ramblers and very convenient for the Heart of England Way.

Map: OS Pathfinder 975 Redditch and Henley-in-Arden

Terrain: an early hill ascent but otherwise easy

Before starting your walk, spare time to meander the colourful High Street in **Henley-in-Arden**. This Britain in Bloom winner offers floral beauty in the summer months and will provide plenty of scenes for your camera.

Start the walk from the timber-framed Guildhall and church in the High Street and walk Beaudesert Lane over the River Alne to reach Beaudesert Church. At the end of the churchyard, proceed through a metal gate and follow the Heart of England Way markers as you commence a steep but short ascent to the top of The Mount. From here you will enjoy fine views over the town and the surrounding countryside. Proceed in a north-east direction on the clear path over the old earthworks of the former castle of the de

Montforts, climbing to reach a pair of stiles in the field corner. Here, leave the Heart of England Way by going over the stile to the right, initially walking the right edge of a field then bearing left to go over a stile to a lane in Kite Green.

Go left at the lane and continue as it arcs to the right. Where the lane bends sharp left, continue ahead (at the public footpath sign) to go through a metal gate on the left and proceed up a tarmac drive. Go over the stile to the right of the next gate and walk a narrow, hedged path. You will pass by a house on your left and a metal fence as you continue into the next field. About halfway over this field go left and aim for a mid-hedge stile. Go over this stile and maintain your line as you walk

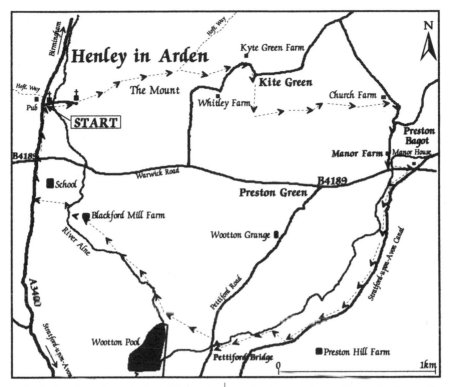

to the left edge of several fields and going over several stiles. Aim towards the buildings of Church Farm, which come into view directly ahead. Proceed to the gate set to the right of the farm buildings.

Go through the gate to a lane. Now go right and walk down the lane, passing by Manor Farm on your left before you reach the B4189 Henley to Warwick road. Go left along the road for about 200 metres, where you will see the attractive russet-coloured and half-timbered 16th-century Preston Bagot Manor House. Cross over the B4189, just after the Warwick Road Bridge, and now descend to the towpath of the Stratford-upon-Avon Canal via a

gate. Proceed south-west along the canal towpath for the next 1¼ miles (2km). This pleasant stretch of towpath walking continues until you reach the second canal bridge, with Preston Hill Farm on your left. Cross the bridge and walk the tarmac track/lane opposite. In 175 metres this bends sharp left and soon you will arrive at a road near to the Pettiford Bridge. Here, go right over the bridge, and in some 45 metres go left over a stile into pastureland. Bear right to diagonally cross the field and to go over a stile in its far left corner and to meet the River Alne.

Walk the riverside path, going generally north-east with Blackford Mill Farm prominent ahead. You

The Guild Hall and Church in Henley-in-Arden

will go over a couple of footbridges before reaching a division of paths. Here, bear left to stay fairly near to the river and to go through a gate set to the far left of the farm complex. Cross the footbridge over the River Alne and walk a narrow path ahead by a fence until you reach a stile. Go over the stile and cross the school playing fields to a final stile that leads to the A3400.

Go right and walk the pavement of the A3400 into Henley-in-Arden. If you have not previously meandered the town you will have the opportunity of seeing many of the floral displays draping the shops as you approach the Guildhall prior to returning to your car.

Walk 12: Alcester and the Bluebell Wood

This walk takes you through one of the most attractive bluebell woods in Warwickshire and provides the opportunity to spend time in historic and colourful Alcester.

Distance: 5 miles (8km); **Duration:** 3 hours

Car Parking: Park in the free municipal car park in Bleachfield Street, at the rear of The Swan Hotel, Alcester (SP 088573).

Refreshments: The Swan Hotel is a 16th-century coaching inn which played a major role in the 19th century in servicing coaches to Birmingham, Stratford-upon-Avon and Evesham. Today the hotel specialises in home-cooked foods and welcomes walkers with an inexpensive three-course lunch menu.

Map: OS Pathfinder 997 Stratford-upon-Avon (West) and Alcester

Terrain: Easy

From the Bleachfield Street car park, go left pass The Swan Hotel and cross over the Old Stratford Road at the pedestrian crossing to walk the High Street of attractive **Alcester**. Spare time to meander the medieval streets, including Butter Street by the church, and visit the old town hall. When you are ready, continue with the walk by proceeding down the delightful Malt Mill Lane, perhaps accepting the invitation of the local residents to meander through their beautiful gardens. At the bottom of the lane look back for a fine photo opportunity.

Continue down Malt Mill Lane to reach a car parking area. Go left through lawned gardens by the side of the River Alne and through a gateway to the pavement of the Old Stratford Road. Cross the road with care and proceed down the lane opposite, passing Alcester football ground and then crossing the bridge over the River Arrow to enter the village of Oversley Green. Bear left at the road junction, and in about 75 metres go right to walk a footpath which initially goes over a field and then becomes a hedged path behind a row of houses and a golf driving range. At a junction of paths go right (south-east), crossing a field to go over a stile then bearing left to continue in a east-south-east direction. Pass near to Oversley Hill Farm before going over a stile near to an electric sub-station set near (and below) to the A46.

Proceed under the road bridge and bear right to enter Oversley Wood via a kissing gate. You now walk the woodland track through the attractive wood, which is a picture of bluebells in spring each year. The track proceeds south-west for about over three-quarters of a mile (1.4km) then bends left and arcs round until you are actually starting to walk in a north-east direction. About 350 metres on, bear right on a track which allows you to exit the wood. Rosehall Farm should be visible. As

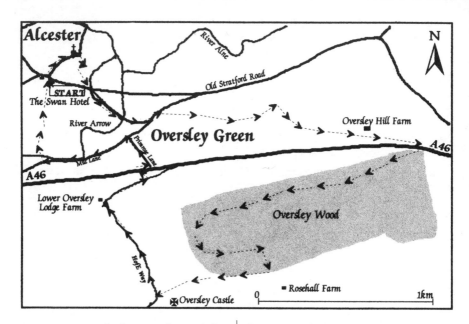

soon as you exit the wood, go right along the wood-edge and continue ahead at the end of the wood, maintaining the walk line on a hedged track. When the tree hedge ends you will be rewarded with a good view of the white, castellated Oversley Castle set on the hill to the left. You will soon reach a farm lane. Turn right along the lane to join the Heart of England Way.

Walk this farm lane for the next three-quarters of a mile (1.2km). Looking to your left you will see Ragley Hall sited on the hill over the River Arrow. Continue to the right of Lower Oversley Lodge Farm and its massive grain silos and you will have a fine view over the town of Alcester. Descend the lane and go left over a stile to walk over the footbridge over the busy A46. On the other side of the bridge you will enter Primrose Lane, passing by a beautiful thatched

house and descending to reach a T-junction by further fine thatched properties in Oversley Green. Go left along Mill Lane for about 600 metres then, just before reaching a residential caravan site, go right down a path to cross over a pedestrianised bridge over the River Arrow. The path becomes more of a track then a lane by residential houses with allotments to the right. Continue into Bleachfield Street in **Alcester** and soon you will reach the town car park at the back of The Swan Hotel.

Walk 13: Bidford Riverside Walk and the Cottage of Content

A walk along the banks of the River Avon.

Distance: 4 miles (6km); **Duration:** 2 to 2½ hours

Car Parking: At The Cottage of Content Pub in Barton (SP 107513) or in the free public car park by the road island in Bidford (SP 099519)

Refreshments: A 17th-century pub which in 1850 was kept by a blacksmith and described as Barton Public House, The Cottage of Content is now a regular watering hole for local walkers.

Maps: OS Pathfinder Maps 997 Stratford-upon-Avon (West) and Alcester, and 1020 Vale of Evesham

Terrain: Easy walking

Start from The Cottage of Content at Barton. Leave the pub, going right along the B4085 for 100 metres. Where the road bends sharp right, proceed ahead up a lane towards Barton Farm. About 150 metres from the road, go right leaving the lane (and the Heart of England Way) and continuing on a green track which ascends south-west then arcs right to the right of a hedge fence. Walk this path for a little more than half a mile then go right over a stile. Now proceeding in a south-easterly direction, join the farm drive to Bickmarsh Hall Farm. You will pass to the right of this major farm complex and soon reach the main road. Go right along the grass verge of the road, passing by the roadside houses in Bickmarsh to go left along Bickmarsh Lane.

Walk Bickmarsh Lane for its length and you will arrive in the hamlet of Marlcliff. Along the way you will pass by houses in Bickmarsh before reaching cultivated farmland. A fine view of the surrounding countryside will unfold as you descend to the road junction in Marlcliff. Now go right along the B4085 for some 80 metres then go left to stroll an attractive lane into the centre of the hamlet. Where the dead-end lane bends right, continue ahead (east). Pass by a delightful, tiny thatched cottage and the corner house called 'Woodpeckers' as you proceed down a green lane towards the River Avon.

Just before the river go right over a stile and walk the Avon Valley Footpath on the bank of the River Avon. You will go over a couple of stiles before arriving in the recreation ground, which you will exit by the Bidford on Avon Bridge. Go left over the fine old bridge and then right to spend time meandering the attractive town centre of **Bidford-on-Avon**. When you have had your fill of the town, retrace your steps back to the bridge and cross back over again.

At the end of the bridge, go left over a stile to continue with the walk along the Heart of England Way over

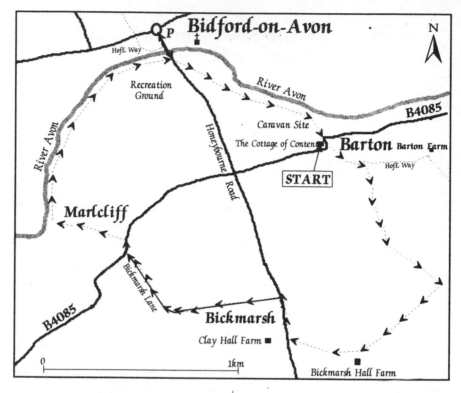

pastureland, sparing time to enjoy the river view by the bridge and the half-timbered building by the fine church. The path diagonally crosses three fields, going over stiles as you proceed in a south-west direction. You will soon be walking the bank of the Avon with a weir and lock forming a pleasing picture to your left. As you near the lock, go right into a hedged green lane and proceed through a gate to reach the B4085 once again, at a road corner with The Cottage of Content on your right.

Walk 14: Hidcote Manor Hill Walk

Good views of the pleasing Cotswold landscape are here combined with an opportunity to visit the famous Hidcote Manor Gardens (NT).

Distance: 5 miles (8km); **Duration:** 3 hours

Car Parking: Park your car by the roadside in Mickleton.

Refreshments: The King's Arms Inn is an old coaching inn which has become a regular eating house for local walkers. You will be made very welcome.

Map: OS Pathfinder 1020 Vale of Evesham

Terrain: One early ascent, otherwise easy

Leave your car in **Mickleton** in the small parking area near to St Lawrence's Church. Commence the walk by crossing the lane, and going left then right up a grass slope immediately after the drive to Field House, following a signed path. Proceed through a kissing gate and walk a field to a gate in its far right corner.

Walk the path through the trees to a further gate, then climb gently to the left side of a field to reach a gate. Here, go right to join the Heart of England Way and uphill to a gate to a lane near Baker's Hill. Pause here for a fine view of Mickleton then cross the lane and ascend the stepped path through trees to a stile. Go right along Baker's Hill, with trees to the right, before entering the wood. Follow the track inside the edge of the wood; walk to its end, then cross a field and bear left around a barn/farm buildings to reach a narrow lane. Go right along the lane for about 400 metres to reach Furze Lane, passing Starveall Farm and with Knowles Coppice on the right.

Go left along Furze Lane (leaving the Heart of England Way) for about 220 metres then go left again through a gate to a path that arcs north-east to a stile. It then crosses a second field

to a further stile on to Hidcote Road. Here, pause to look back over the Cotswold Hills with Broadway Tower at the crest, then go left along the road for about 100 metres. Go right at the crossroads and meander through the sleepy and pretty hamlet of Hidcote Boyce – a real pleasure when the flowers of spring are at their peak. Proceed to Top Farm and go through a kissing gate. Go diagonally left over the field on a clear path to a further stile. Heading north, continue on the path along the edge of a very large field. There is a fruit farm to your left as you reach a gateway to a lane in Hidcote Batrim. Walk down the road of this picturesque village of thatched sandstone buildings, passing a 1918 war memorial, the village duck pond and the entrance to Hidcote Manor. Go left at the junction of lanes and walk down the entrance drive, going west for some 200 metres to Hidcote Road. Cross the road and go through a gate to the left of Kiftsgate Court (the finger-post is intended for Mickleton but the ravages of time or vandals have reduced the word to 'ETO'). Diagonally descend a field. The Court building is on your right and the Old Coppice on the left.

Descend to a gap at the bottom and go south into the park. The path arcs right as it descends to a gate and reaches a junction of paths. Continue ahead, following Heart of England Way markers until the car park near to the church. For the King's Arms pub, proceed down the lane into the village of **Mickleton**. You will soon arrive at the B4081 (Chipping Campden to Stratford-upon-Avon road). Here, go left and the King's Arms is on your left. To return to your car, proceed past the King's Arms, going towards Chipping Campden. In a few yards go left up a lane in front of Honeysuckle Cottage, then veer left between two white, period cottages to a fenced path. This path will take you behind the pub and leads behind houses to reach the front of the church of St Lawrence.

Walk 15: Mickleton and the Meon Hill Tour

You will be able to enjoy fine views on this walk and can meander the attractive Cotswold village of Mickleton.

Distance: 6¼ miles (10km); **Duration:** 4 hours

Car Parking: Park by St Lawrence's Church in Mickleton SP 159434.

Refreshments: The King's Arms, Mickleton provides a good snack menu which is a favourite with local rambling groups – you will be made very welcome

Map: OS Pathfinder 1020 Vale of Evesham

Terrain: A fairly easy walk with some undulations.

From St Lawrence's Church, **Mickleton** go left (south-east), passing through a small gate into a field to walk the Heart of England Way. Cross over the field to go through a second gate to the left of a hedge and a narrow copse. Continue meandering in and out of the trees and gently bearing right. Where the Heart of England Way goes right, continue ahead on a clear path that arcs left as it ascends the park of Kiftsgate Court. This delightful ascent ends at a gate leading to a road. Cross over to walk the lane opposite leading up to the car park of Hidcote Manor. Proceed across the car park and then go left over a stile and onto pastureland.

Continue on the path, generally north-east, over a couple of fields and stiles to Hidcote Combe and enjoy the pleasant Cotswold scene. Bear left, then right to go over a stile into a plantation of trees with the valley to the left below. Continue on a clear path through the trees. Leave via a second stile to cross further attractive pasture before going over another stile into woodland by Ash Holts. After leaving the woodland over a stile, bear gently left over a further stile with the hedges closing in

from each side. At the field-end, go left over a small footbridge and a stile into Adminton Lane.

Go right along the lane for about 400 metres then, just before the buildings of Admington Lane Farm, go left over a stile to join the Centenary Way. Follow the waymarkers of the Centenary Way as the path continues in a general north-west direction. Go over a footbridge and through a small gate before going up a field to reach a lane by Homeleigh Cottage via a stile. Go right along the lane for about 50 metres, then go left to walk the drive towards **Meon Hall**. In some 300 metres, just before reaching the hall, go right over stiles to walk parkland. Head in a general north-west direction with a fine view of Meon Hill to your left. As you reach the brow of the hill a superb view of the area unfolds, with Upper Quinton in the foreground.

At the field end go through a gate and bear right to a double stile. Now go left and walk to the left of the field's top hedge. Pass over a further stile to cross diagonally to go over a stile on the edge of Upper Quinton. Now go right to walk by trees then go left over a couple of stiles to arrive

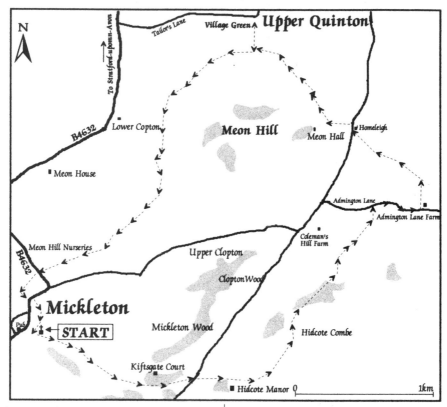

between houses and to reach the village road. If you have time, walk to the right and visit a large village green area where a wooden seat indicates the end of the Centenary Way.

From the village green continue south along the road towards Meon Hill. Rejoin the Heart of England Way and bear right over a stile to enter a field to the right of a cottage. Follow the clear waymarkings on a path which arcs left, generally following the hill contour to the west of Meon Hill, going over a series of fields and stiles. In about 1¼ miles (2km) the path bears right to go over a footbridge and a further stile, passing be-

tween derelict glasshouses before reaching the B4632 in Mickleton.

Cross the B4632 and go over the stile opposite, aiming for a further stile in the field's far left corner. When over the stile, go immediately left and proceed between shops to reach the B4632 once again near the centre of the village of Mickleton. Go left for 25 metres then **cross** the road to walk the lane opposite. This soon reaches a kissing gate where it becomes a footpath, bearing right by a ha-ha wall. At its end, go through a further kissing gate into the churchyard and you will emerge near the car park by the church.

Walk 16: Chipping Campden and Dover's Hill

A meander around beautiful Chipping Campden and then a walk to see the superb views from historic Dover's Hill. On a clear day one can see for miles.

Distance: 5½ miles (9km); **Duration:** 3 to 3½ hours

Car Parking: Park with consideration by the roadside in Calf Lane, Chipping Campden (GR 152391).

Refreshments: The Volunteer Inn, Lower High Street, Chipping Campden is a traditional Cotswold stone pub. The cosy lounge attracts the regular attendance of local walkers.

Maps: OS Pathfinder 1020 Vale of Evesham, and Outdoor Leisure 45 The Cotswolds

Terrain: Undulating

Commence the walk on the Heart of England Way from St James's Church in **Chipping Campden**. Walk down Church Street and go left along the main High Street, which soon becomes Lower High Street and reaches St Catherine's Church. (You will have left the Way as you passed the Noel Arms pub.) Here, go right and walk up Back Ends, following the Cotswold Way waymarkers. In about 30 metres bear left up the bridle path of Hoo Lane and climb the gentle slope to the T-junction at Kingcombe Lane. Here, turn left, cross the lane and then go right up a path with the hedge to the right (pausing to look back to see Chipping Camden behind you).

Bear right at a stile between two ash trees, but pause to enjoy the wide view of the escarpment amphitheatre of Dover's Hill and the Vale of Evesham. If you have time, a walk along the length of Dover's Hill is, on a good clear day, rewarded with a magnificent panorama embracing the Malvern and Bredon Hills. In the

distance the Shropshire hills may be seen. As you proceed right over two fields, walking in a generally north-east direction, the view continues to dominate but soon you will reach the B4035 (Aston Subedge to Chipping Campden road). Cross this road and go through the gate opposite to enter a wood called The Dingle. Go left down the slope on a path that bends right for about 400 metres to a gate.

Go through the gate and in 10 metres go over a stile on the left. Walk to the left of a hedge and a stream across two fields, heading for a stile and copse. Aim for the stile to the left of the copse and go over this onto the B4632 Broadway road. Go right and ascend this road for 400 metres before going right onto a bridleway.

Proceed along this bridleway, going south-east over several fields, with the hedge on your left. You will reach the top of a hill (known as Dairy Hills) and a stile. Go over the stile and continue on a track over

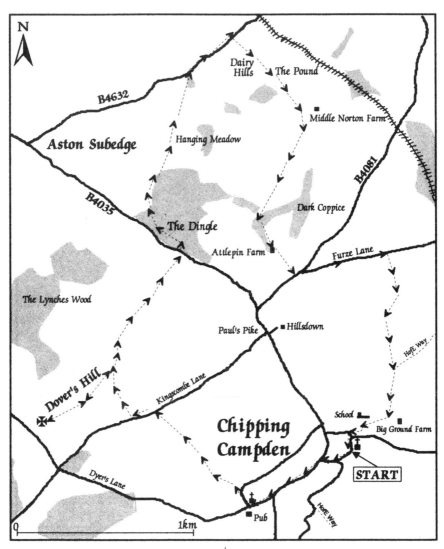

fields with trees to your right. Go over a further stile and diagonally over the next field, with Middle Norton Farm to your left, aiming for a stile in the far corner. Then proceed over three more fields, climbing towards the trees, which you enter over a cattle grid. Bear left along the track through the trees and join a metalled road. As you emerge from the trees you will pass Attlepin Farm (on your right) to reach the B4081 (Mickleton to Chipping Campden road) at its junction with Furze Lane.

Cross over into Furze Lane and walk along it for some 500 metres. Go

The Woolstaplers' Hall in Chipping Campden

right to a footpath, proceed over a stile and walk to the right of the hedge to cross a footbridge over a stream. Go diagonally right and follow the edge of the field to some farm buildings. Then veer left, generally aiming ahead towards the school buildings as you rejoin the Heart of England Way on its route into **Chipping Campden**. Go right at the end of the school playing fields to walk a narrow, hedged path along the front of the school. You will soon arrive at a kissing gate onto the school road. Go left to reach the B4035 by the churchyard. Cross the road and go right along the pavement to return to the church gates and your starting point.

Walk 17: Broad Campden Caper

A short walk through typical undulating Cotswold countryside with superb views over the most attractive village of Broad Campden.

Distance: 3 miles (5km); **Duration:** 2 hours

Car Parking: Park in the car park at the Baker's Arms. Please let the landlord know and he will be pleased to direct you to a convenient part of the parking area SP 157378.

Refreshments: The Baker's Arms pub was built at the end of the 16th century when it was occupied as a bakehouse. In 1720 it was converted to a pub and today it is a traditional Cotswold country pub, offering real ales and good food in a friendly atmosphere.

Map: OS Outdoor Leisure 45 The Cotswolds

Terrain: Easy, with a couple of undulations

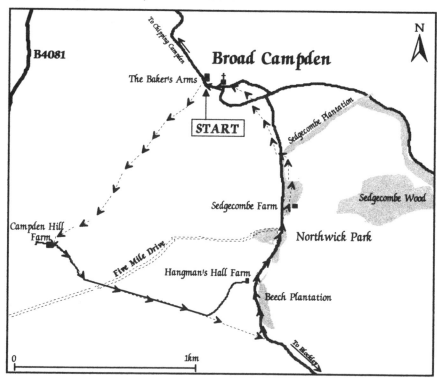

Cross the road in front of the Baker's Arms and proceed through the gate to the right of a wall to join the Heart of England Way. Continue in a south-west direction, walking diagonally over the large field and aiming for a stile in its far right-hand corner.

Go over the stile and continue on the same direction line, climbing to the top of the field and passing to the right of a small fenced area. Now walk the clear path by the hill wall/fence, going over a couple of stiles and then bearing right to reach a small gate with Campden Hill Farm ahead. Go through the gate and proceed to the left of the farm buildings to reach a farm lane via a second small gate. Go left and walk this fine Cotswold stone lane as it ascends south-east to reach Five Mile Drive. Proceed through the trees on the drive and continue on the lane to the left of a hedge – you will arrive in a small copse. Go through the copse until you reach a gate (on the right) and leave the Heart of England Way by going left and descending to the Chipping Campden to Blockley road.

Go left and walk the lane, with Beech Plantation on your right. After about 250 metres you will pass the entrance to Hangman's Hall Farm (on your

left), and then in a further 350 metres you will reach the entrance to Northwich Park on the right. Go right on the entrance road and then immediately left over a stile into Sedgecombe Plantation. Walk north on the clear path through the plantation and in 400 metres go left over a stile to the road once again. There is a viewing seat here for you to rest while you enjoy a superb view over Broad Campden below.

Cross the road and go over the stile opposite to enjoy that beautiful view as you descend the hill towards Broad Campden. Aim for a stile in the middle of the hedge below, which you go over to reach the main road in the village. Cross the road and continue down the hedged footpath opposite. This leads behind gardens and proceeds over a small bridge before you climb the path to reach the road again in front of St Michael's Church. Proceed up the road and you will find the Baker's Arms on the right, just round the corner.

The Bakers Arms, Broad Campden

Walk 18: Beautiful Blockley

An enchanting walk over undulating countryside around the beautiful Cotswold village of Blockley. There are magnificent views of the town at the end of the walk.

Distance: 4 miles (6km); **Duration:** 2 to 2½ hours

Car Parking: You can park in the small free car park (toilets) in Blockley GR 164350.

Refreshments: The Great Western Arms was originally one of two houses (the other was used as a blacksmith's) which were converted to a pub in 1900 for workers building the local railway. The line, used as a siding sending elm boards to London and Birmingham for coffin manufacture, was closed in 1966. Today the pub is a very popular watering house for the local ramblers and you will be made very welcome.

Map: OS Outdoor Leisure 45 The Cotswolds

Terrain: Easy, with a couple of undulations

Leave **Blockley** by exiting the churchyard at its rear and climbing left up Bell Bank into Bucks End. Proceed along Chapel Lane to cross over Greenway Road. Now go up between houses to a stile and cross a cultivated field to a gap in its far hedge. Continue over a stile into a field with five large trees in a row on its brow. Go right in front of the trees, aiming towards a stile near the last house on the Chipping Campden road to Blockley.

Go left on the road then cross to go over a further stile to the left of a farm gateway. Follow the direction of footpath waymarks, aiming towards the far left-hand corner of the large field. Go over this stile and a small railway sleeper footbridge to walk by the side of a wide, tree hedge and to go over another stile to a farm lane. Go right along this lane to reach the B4479, known as Station Road. Cross the road and proceed down the driveway opposite. Here you can ad-

mire a fine terrace of 1837 Cotswold cottages – known as Mill Row. Proceed past the cottages on the well-maintained driveway into a very attractive private garden with an ornamental pond. Go ahead, (keeping to the footpath) over a stile situated to the left of the private garage. Continue, bearing left by the side of Blockley Brook with Northwick Mill on the other side of the stream. Follow the waymark signs over two further stiles to a road. Cross the road to proceed over another stile and then to ascend diagonally right to a track into the village of Draycott. Proceed up this track, going to the right of Draycott Home Farm and passing a new housing development. Go right after the last of the new houses and walk the village road between pleasing Cotswold cottages and passing the Draycott Mission building to reach a crossroads. Here, go ahead up the lane signed 'Batsford 1½ Moreton-in-Marsh 2½'.

Blockley church

Oldborough Farm to go over a stile onto the farm drive. Cross over the drive and proceed on the footpath to the left and on the other side of the hedge to the farmhouse via a footbridge/stile – it goes along the side of the field and the stream to a further footbridge/stile. Now go right over this second footbridge/stile and commence an ascent of the impressive hill ahead, aiming towards a stile in the top right-hand corner of the field. Continue to climb over the next two fields to a stile at the top, where you should pause to enjoy a splendid view of Draycott and the surrounding countryside. You may also wish to recover your breath after the 90-metre ascent before proceeding to climb the next field to a gate. Go through the gate and cross a bridleway track to go over a stile to a clear pathway through a fine avenue

You will pass The Old Chequers B&B and then, immediately after Landgate House, go right over a stile which leads along the back of the houses in the village. In about 150 metres go left over the cultivated field, aiming just to the left of

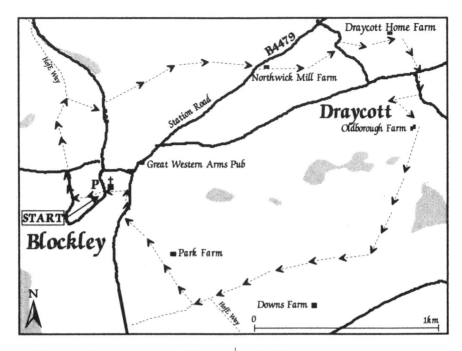

of old oak and sycamore trees. This is a very fine walk of some 800 metres, where you can enjoy a fine view over Blockley and the surrounding Cotswold villages. Walk this path to a gate where you will join the Heart of England Way and follow its waymarks into Blockley. In 100 metres go right over a stile into a sheep field and descend the hill into **Blockley**. A magnificent view unfolds in front of you, with the village church standing proud - you will be enthralled by the view as you go over two more stiles to arrive on a wide track which descends to a village road. Go right and in about 150 metres go left to climb a narrow path that leads into the churchyard where you started the walk.

Walk 19: Lower Swell and Stow-on-the-Wold

An easy town walk in timeless Stow-on-the-Wold together with a visit to the nearby picturesque Cotswold village of Lower Swell – there are fine views over lovely countryside to enjoy.

Distance: 4 miles (6km); **Duration:** 2½ hours

Car Parking: Park in the free car park (with toilets) opposite the Bell Inn in Maugersbury Road, off the A436 in Stow on the Wold (GR 196256).

Refreshments: The Bell Inn or one of many eating houses in Stow on the Wold

Map: OS Outdoor Leisure 45 The Cotswolds

Terrain: Easy

Leave the car park in **Stow-on-the-Wold** and proceed east into Park Street and then Sheep Street, passing antique and dolls shops to reach the main A429 Cirencester to Morton-in-Marsh road. Go left and walk down the pavement of the Fosse Way for nearly 800 metres then cross the busy road (with great care) to enter a

track opposite signed to Lower Swell. With a farm complex to your left, proceed through a farm gate to walk an enclosed track that leads along the left-hand edge of a coppice and then go over a stile to enter a field. Pause to enjoy a pleasant view towards Guiting Power, then proceed to a stile in the hedge opposite. Go over the stile and walk through

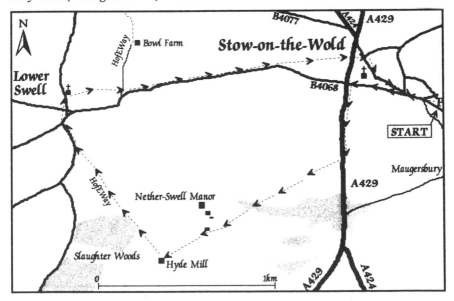

woodland to a gate. Walk through paddocks by the side of a fence/hedge and then go through two white gates that lead to the left of Nether Swell Manor buildings and to a further gate. Pass through this gate and go diagonally across a field of horses to reach a smart white gate in the field's bottom corner – alternatively you may use the clearly signed alternative permissive path which is set to the right of the gate and goes around the edge of the field. Proceed through this bottom gate and veer right to walk over a planked bridge over the stream to the rear of Hyde Mill – a very old building which is believed to have been referred to in the Domesday Book as ' Hide Mill'. ('Hide' related to the medieval rating system measuring value.) The privately owned pond is a home for waterfowl and is an attractive sight from the bridge.

Cross over the bridge and bear left around the buildings then bear right to join the Heart of England Way as it aims north-west. Go through an iron gate and follow the bridleway signs over the next field to a further gate and bridge, keeping Slaughter Woods on your left. The path becomes a wide track between wired fences for about 800 metres and there are views over Nether Swell Manor to your far right. At the track end proceed through a gate on the left to a stone-walled track. At the end of the walled track, go right onto a lane that leads into Lower Swell. There is a farm complex on your right and you will pass by several attractive Cotswold cottages.

Bear right into **Lower Swell** then veer left to cross a road junction at the village centre and to go up a metalled road ahead towards the superb village church. Go through a stile to the right of the church then veer right across the village field to a stile to a lane near the main entrance gate to Abbotswood Estate. Here, go right on to the B4068 and climb towards Stow-on-the-Wold for about 800 metres. Go left through a kissing gate to climb a field to a gate which leads to a hedged track and then to the A429 Fosse Way road. Cross the road with care and enter a passageway to the left of Stow Youth Centre. It leads past toilets into the very attractive town centre of Stow-on-the-Wold. Take time to enjoy this very pleasant town and perhaps imbibe at one of the many old inns. Depart the town centre down Digbeth Street to Park Street and the A436 to return to your car.

Walk 20: Bourton-on-the-Water and Lower Slaughter Delight

A delightful walk to Lower Slaughter, one of the most attractive villages in the Cotswolds. There are fine views on this gentle ramble as you meander by rivers and streams and through pleasant woodland before strolling along the banks of the Windrush on the return to picturesque Bourton-on-the-Water.

Distance: 4 miles (6km); **Duration:** 2½ hours

Car Parking: Station Road Pay and Display car park (toilets) In Bourton-on-the-Water GR 170208

Refreshments: Bourton-on-the-Water has many pubs and cafés. The Coach and Horses on the A429 may be convenient.

Maps: OS Landranger 163 Cheltenham and Cirencester, and Pathfinder 1067 Stow-on-the-Wold

Terrain: Easy

The old mill at Lower Slaughter

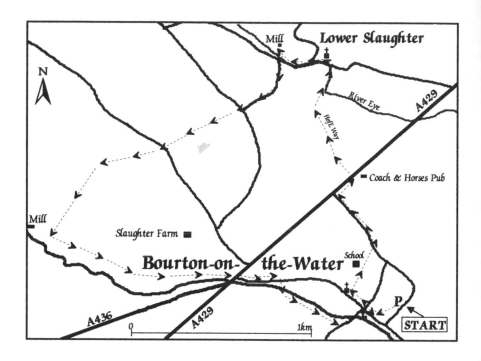

Leave the car park in Station Road, **Bourton-on-the-Water** and walk the path towards the town then go right to walk a tarmac footpath at the back of the shops and houses. Cross over a side road and continue on the path at the back of attractive cottages then go right to walk a clear tarmac lane past school buildings. There are playing fields on both sides. You will soon reach a road and should go left. Walk the pavement of this road for about 400 metres to reach the main A429. Go right along the pavement of this busy road towards the Coach and Horses Inn. In about 90 metres, just before reaching the inn, cross the A429 with great care and proceed left through a kissing-gate to a footpath signed to Lower Slaughter. Walk the

tarmac path through a further gate and continue, soon bearing right with a hedge on the right. Go through a final gate to walk a hedged path with a stream on your left and soon arrive at the main road in the village of Lower Slaughter.

Go left up this road by the side of the very attractive River Eye. Ducks at play will entertain you. Walk by the side of the river, bearing slightly left but keeping to the right of the river past a group of very attractive Cotswold cottages as you walk in the direction of Upper Slaughter. After passing a second picturesque bridge and a lane to the left, bear right to walk to the right of the much-photographed Lower Slaughter Mill.

From the mill return to the main road and cross this to walk the lane that is almost immediately opposite. You will climb past a small, tree-enclosed spring on the right and will soon arrive at a lane. Cross over the lane and walk a clear, fenced bridle path ascending over the brow of the hill – there is a fine view of Bourton-on-the-Water in the valley to your left. This improves after you have passed a walled clump of trees in the field to the left. Cross the next lane and proceed through the gate opposite to diagonally (south-east) cross the cultivated field to a gate in its far right corner. Here go left again and descend through two further gates and past a delightful copse to arrive near to the Windrush. Spare time to go to the right to reach the river and to see a fine Old Mill (now converted to an attractive house) on your right. Now retrace your steps to continue south-east to a clear path into the trees. Soon you will emerge from the trees and can continue on the clear path on the north bank of the river. Proceed over the dismantled railway line and walk along the side of the River Windrush as it winds its way towards a gate leading to the A429 and the town of Bourton-on-the-Water. Go through the gate, cross the busy A429 with care and enter the village. Initially walk along the footpath by the road opposite and then continue on a path between a wall and a line of trees to walk the riverbank. In about 250 metres (just before the Sycamore Guest House) go right over a footbridge to walk on the opposite bank of the river – a most attractive walk at the back of colourful gardens and with open fields to your right. Proceed through a gate, still walking by the banks of the river.

Soon, the path veers to the right and away from the river towards houses and a kissing gate. Go through this gate and along an enclosed path to reach Sherbourne Street, near to a doctors' surgery. Go left between town buildings to reach a road bridge and the High Street in **Bourton-on-the-Water** – this most attractive Venice of the Cotswolds.

Towns and Places of Interest

Alcester

What a delight to walk the streets of ancient Alcester. This winner of the Britain in Bloom competition is a blaze of floral colour in spring and throughout the summer months. It also has a pleasing mix of old, half-timbered buildings along its attractive High Street. Set at the confluence of the rivers Arrow and Alne, the town is at a junction of Roman roads. The Romans first arrived here in about AD47, building a fort to accommodate a military detachment just to the south of the town. Pronounced 'Olster' by local people, the town later became a regular stopping place for travellers and several of the old coaching inns remain. With the Industrial Revolution came engineering, needle-making factories and ironworks but much of this is no longer visible.

Today, Alcester is a small residential town which sports a fine 17th-century town hall, an imposing church with a curiously positioned clock, a beautiful pedestrianised Malt Mill Lane and a fine collection of half-timbered buildings – spare time to meander the old streets of this attractive town.

South of Alcester the walker will pass near the impressive stately home of Ragley Hall – it has a wonderful collection of treasures with a magnificent mural. Capability Brown landscaped the gardens. Two miles north is Coughton Court, the home of the Throckmorton family since 1409. This NT property is rich in history, having close connections with the Gunpowder Plot, the Civil War, Mary Queen of Scots and sanctuary for persecuted priests.

Baddesley Clinton

The tiny village of Baddesley Clinton is dominated by Baddesley Manor House (NT) and a fine church. The 13th-century moated Manor House was the home of the Ferrers family, the most famous of whom was 'the Antiquary' from 1549 to 1633. It is now a National Trust property and still contains a number of priest holes. These were built in the 1590s by Nicholas Owen to hide priests who were being persecuted at the time. Set in beautiful gardens with an attractive moat, the property is well worth a visit. The church of St Michael and All Saints forms an idyllic scene when a carpet of daffodils and bluebells encircles it in the spring. It was closely associated with the Manor House and beneath the chancel floor lie many generations of the Ferrers family. It is believed that the building was first erected in the 11th century, maybe prior to the Conquest. The church contains a fascinating English Chamber Organ inscribed 'Sarah Green, Organ Builder to their Majesties Isleworth 1797'.

Berkswell

As one approaches Berkswell from the south one passes the lake and buildings of Berkswell Hall (renowned for its rhododendron display and now occupied as apartments) and then reaches the superb Norman church with a most unusual two-storeyed, gabled and timbered porch. Obviously this is a rather special village. There are red-roofed and timbered, white cottages and an intriguing set of stocks which legend suggests were built with holes to contain a peg-legged villager and his two companions. The 16th-century Bear Inn was originally called The Bear and Ragged Staff and retains its original open fireplace and its Cromwellian associations. The Berkswell well is a tank of 16sq ft, walled in with stone and set near to the church.

Bidford-on-Avon

Proximity to the River Avon has played a large part in the history of this attractive small town. Once a Roman road crossed by a ford near to the church of St Lawrence (it has a fine medieval tower). An Anglo-Saxon burial ground was dug in 1922, unearthing some 200 Roman warriors and their women. William Shakespeare, who spent many drinking hours in the 16th-century Falcon Inn, regularly visited the town. On occasion he committed his feeling for the locality into verse:

Bidford Bridge

*'Piping Pebworth, Dancing Marston
Haunted Hillborough, Hungry Grafton
Dodging Exhall, Papist Wixford
Beggarly Broom and Drunken Bidford'*

Today a road by-pass has returned the town centre of 15th- and 16th-century houses to relative peace, while the impressive 8-arch bridge (mainly 15th-century) leads to relaxing parkland.

Birmingham and Fazeley Canal

Completed in 1790 to form a link between Birmingham and the south-east, the Bimingham and Fazeley Canal was designed by John Smeaton to accommodate a massive growth in the canal-side industry. Today, like most canals, it is a source of leisure and pleasure.

Blockley

This very old silk village lies to the west of the Fosse Way Roman road and was recorded in the Domesday Book as having several mills and various factories. These included 12 mill-wheels on Blockley Brook, with 500 people employed. Later Blockley became a silk town that supplied Coventry's ribbon manufacturers. One of the old mills can be seen today beyond a pool near the church. In 1780 the village had five silk mills along its streams. It expanded so that in 1880 there were six mills employing 600 workers plus some 3,000 people working from their homes. A few years later the whole business collapsed and over the last century it has reverted to being a peaceful Cotswold village set above the Blockley Brook, which meanders in a

most pleasing way. The terraces of workers' cottages and the houses of the mill owners and managers have been transformed into charming and handsome residences. Blockley, one of the first villages to be lit by electricity (1887), remains an attractive village set on several levels, with narrow streets, steep paths and a fascinating vista of roofs of varying height.

Bourton-on-the-Hill

Bourton-on-the-Hill is a picturesque village sited on a steep hill with an ancient church and rows of cottages set near to the busy A44 Moreton-in-Marsh to Broadway road. Bourton on the Hill still has pleasant quiet backwaters to explore.

This parish was the inheritance and birthplace of the unfortunate Sir Thomas Overbury, whose death by poison in 1613 is recorded in the parish register of the massive church. The register also shows that Sir Nicholas Overbury died in 1643, 'being upwards of 100 years old' and Revd Dr Warneford, the philanthropic clergyman, was buried in the churchyard. The 18th-century Bourton House, at the bottom of the hill, has a superb 16th-century tithe barn that is strongly buttressed and has a tall, gabled porch.

Bourton-on-the-Water

Bourton-on-the-Water was an important place in Roman times. A few furlongs from the village is a Roman camp enclosing about 24 hectares (60 acres), and here 147 swords, coins, pottery, and other vestiges of Roman occupation were discovered.

The church was almost entirely re-built in 1785, but the chancel, which dates from 1328, has some simple but good 14th-century windows and there is also a Victorian nave and a distinctive Georgian tower. At the old Manor House, some paperhangers who were stripping a wall on the landing of the second floor discovered a secret chamber over a century ago. The room, which was only 8ft square, was exactly as the last occupant left it: a teapot and cup that still held a rusty spoon were on the table, and over the back of the only chair hung a priest's black cassock.

Today, Bourton is a very popular, picturesque town. The River Windrush meanders beneath a series of graceful bridges and in December a wide variety of Christmas illuminations add to the scenic splendour of the town. Apart from its visual impact, Bourton has a number of other attractions for the visitor. The town is a Mecca for children with Birdland, a model village, a motor museum, a perfume factory and a model railway.

Cannock Chase

Once the hunting ground of Plantagenet kings, this 26 square miles of protected moorland and forest is classified as one of Britain's Areas of Outstanding Natural Beauty. One thousand years ago, giant oak trees covered much of the area and a stranger (a walker) would probably have got lost within minutes. Today, there is a clear network of tracks over the Chase and there are several good viewing places along the lovely walking routes. German

The Motor Museum at Bourton-on-the-Water

and Commonwealth war cemeteries can be found on the Chase – the graves of the first Zeppelin crew shot down over Britain during the First World War can be seen in the German cemetery.

Castle Ring

Castle Ring is the highest point on Cannock Chase at 801ft (224 metres). An extensive Iron Age fort with well-preserved ramparts and ditches provides extensive views over the Trent Valley.

Chipping Campden

This old wool town is full of Cotswold stone buildings: a 15th-century church and a 17th-century Market Hall being but two of its buildings worthy of inspection. Next to the Woolstaplers Hall is a stone denoting the end of the Cotswold Way from Bath. The church is a wool church, evidence of the town's prosperity in the 'Golden Age' of the Cotswold wool trade. Below the church there is a row of almshouses (1612) leading to the Market Hall 1627. The town is full of interest – and antique shops!

Donnington Brewery

The well-known Donnington Brewery is set in a picturesque 14th-century building surrounded by pleasing gardens. It was once a thriving corn mill and later used by cloth weavers. It produces real ale and has a small string of local Donnington public houses. The ale has a fine reputation in the area.

Drayton Bassett

Drayton Bassett was the birthplace of Sir Robert Peel, the Prime Minister and father of our police force. He is buried in the village churchyard.

Cottages in Broad Campden

Drayton Manor park does not exist any more. The park has become a golf course and the Drayton Manor Park and Zoo. The zoo occupies several acres of park and has a wide selection of animals. There is also a large amusement park and a lake.

Grand Union Canal

Prior to becoming the Grand Union Canal, the waterway was the Warwick and Birmingham Canal. To provide a major trading artery from London (Berkhamstead) to Birmingham the old canal was widened and extended and eight different canals were linked to form The Grand Union Canal in 1929.

Henley-in-Arden

The medieval High Street in Henley-in-Arden is one of the best known in England. It is rich in fine architecture and has many black and white half-timbered buildings to admire. It is believed that the poet Shenstone was inspired by the 16th-century White Swan coaching inn when writing 'the warmest welcome at an inn'. The De Montfort family has long connections with the small town. He built a motte and bailey castle on the Mount in the 12th century and the town is believed to have been a trading centre for his stronghold. Sadly, the Beaudesert Castle no longer exists but the walk over The Mount remains a treat for any walker. The 15th-century Guildhall is the home of the Court Leat, who add to the floral colour of this Britain in Bloom winning town.

Kingsbury Water Park

The lakes in Kingsbury Water Park were created by the extraction of gravel over a period of 50 years until 1975. Some of the pits filled with water naturally while others were landscaped to produce 30 attractive lakes. Today the attractive water park offers some 240 hectares (600 acres) of beautiful waterside walking with fishing pools, a boating lake, a nature trail through woodland and a large range of wildlife habitat.

Lichfield

Take time to meander the medieval grid street pattern of the ancient city of Lichfield. Visit the unique sandstone cathedral with its three wonderful spires (known as 'the Ladies of the Vale') and see the Georgian house of Dr Samuel Johnson, the famous 18th-century writer and personality. Stroll the delightful small city, walk the Minster Pool and admire the striking red brick and stucco buildings that line the old streets.

Longborough

Here there is a delightful road of Cotswold stone cottages. Several have been converted from old farm buildings and other display their origins such as the 'Old Bake-house'. The Coach and Horse Inn is a Donnington pub selling only drinks.

Lower Slaughter

Take your camera to this picturesque Cotswold village lying beside the little River Eye – it has a delightful duck/trout stream which meanders under bridges and through the village. Lower Slaughter is a village beloved by artists who are attracted by a mixture of the stream, cottages and the superb old mill at the western end. The beautiful village inspired William Allingham to write, 'Four ducks on a pond, A grassy bank beyond: A blue sky of spring, White clouds on the wing What a little thing To remember for years – To remember with tears.'

Lower Swell

The village of Lower Swell has many interesting features. The Spa House, at the foot of the hill, was built in 1807 and is so named because of a chalybeate spring. Three bells are a visible feature of the church, which also has a Saxon door, a Norman porch with rare mouldings and a tympanum of the Tree of Life with a bird beneath its boughs. There are several barrows on the down and two ancient Druidical stones – the Whittlestone and the Hoarstone. Spare time to meander this delightful unspoilt village. Nearby, Abbotswood House, erected in 1867, is a mansion in the Elizabethan style.

Meon Hill

On Meon Hill there is an extensive camp of British origin which is supposed to have been subsequently used by the West Saxons before the engagement between themselves and the Mercians near Campden. Extensive views are obtained from its fertile summit.

Mickleton

The village of Mickleton, called 'Mycclantune' by the Saxons, is more of that period than are the surrounding villages. The church, decorated with portions of Norman and Perpendicular, consists of a nave, two aisles, and a spire of elegant proportions. It contains many monuments for the families of Fisher and Graves, among which is one to the memory of Richard Graves, an eminent historian and antiquary who died in 1729. His collections are included in the British Museum. The Manor House, purchased by another Richard Graves, a lawyer of repute under the Commonwealth, adjoins the churchyard. Sir A. Keck, a Lord Commissioner of the Great Seal in 1688, was born here in 1630.

Meander this pleasant village and take time to enjoy its fine pubs.

The Kings Arms, Mickleton

Three Ways House Hotel is the home of the famous Pudding Club where clients visit on a regular basis to enjoy an evening of exotic puddings. Near to the hotel is a water fountain with an interesting memorial, 'The water was brought into this village in the year 1875 and the fountain built in memory of Sir J.M. Steele Graves Bart and of his daughter Mrs Bowen Graves who lie in the churchyard of this Parish.' Nearby are the famous National Trust Gardens of Hidcote Manor – 4 hectares (10 acres) of gardens created in the early 20th century by Major Lawrence Johnson. In summer the six major gardens are a very popular attraction, with fine views to the west from the top of the garden over the valley to Bredon Hill.

Milford

This tiny hamlet marks the end of the Heart of England Way. Its common is a popular place with weekend visitors as it provides easy access to Cannock Chase.

Moreton-in-Marsh

A small Cotswold market town which consists of one wide street nearly half a mile long. This broad street is built on the Fosse Way and was originally the crossroads of four counties – the word 'marsh' is a corruption of 'march' meaning a boundary. The 13th-century church of St David possesses some fine Elizabethan plate and a Winchester Bushel and Peck. There are a number of good 17th- and 18th-century houses lining the honey-coloured street. The handsome Redesdale Hall is a centrepiece. The Curfew Tower is sited opposite to the Market Hall and contains an original curfew bell that was tolled up until 1860. The Redesdale Arms is an old coaching inn. The town's railway was one to escape the Beeching Axe.

Packwood House

Built in the Tudor period with restorations in the 17th century, Packwood House is now owned by the National Trust. The building contains interesting period furniture, with Jacobean panelling and an original over-mantel in the Ireton Room. John Fetherstone built the stables before 1666, and he also planted the Yew Garden at Packwood House. The nearby 13th-century church of St Giles contains a register record of the marriage between Michael Johnson of Lichfield and Sarah Ford.

Sezincote

Sezincote House is an impressive oriental-style building which was built by Sir Charles Cockerell in 1805, after he served a spell in India. Its style influenced the Prince Regent who built the Brighton Pavilion in 1812. The house is open Thursdays and Fridays in the summer from 2.30 to 6.00, while the gardens are open on Thursdays, Fridays and Bank Holiday Mondays 2.00 to 6.00. Sezincote village is recorded in the Domesday Book as supporting a plough team of 12. The benefice of its church was moved to the church in the very attractive neighbouring village of Longborough in 1750 and remains there.

Shugborough Hall

This splendid mansion has been the home of the Anson family for about 350 years and has a strong association with Admiral Lord Anson. Set on the edge of Cannock Chase, Shugborough is the home of Thomas Patrick Anson, the 5th Earl of Lichfield, who is better known as Patrick Lichfield the professional photographer of Playboy-calendar fame. The present building was started in 1695, enlarged in the 1700s and 1800s and is today a National Trust property. There is an important collection of 18th-century French furniture. Within the 360-hectare (900-acre) estate there is a remarkable collection of neo-classical garden monuments: A Chinese House, A Cat's Monument, The Shepherd's Monument, A Doric Temple, The Tower of the Winds, The Lantern of Demosthenes and The Triumphal Arch.

Stow-on-the-Wold

This ancient market town is the highest town in the Cotswolds. It is situated by the Fosse Way at an altitude of 750ft (230m), and a local saying is, 'Stow-on-the-Wold, where the winds blow cold.' It was originally built in a wood (hence the word 'wold' meaning 'wood') and a traditional couplet says, 'A squirrel can hop from Swell to Stowe without resting his foot or wetting his toe.' Evesham Abbey founded the town as a market place in the mid-11th century and thousands of sheep were sold here – hence the street names of Sheep Street and Shepherd's Way.

Narrow alleyways for controlling sheep lead off the town square which is the centre of activity and there are a number of interesting mellow Cotswold structures built from stone from the local quarries. The Market Cross is a symbolic reminder to traders to deal with honesty and fairness. Those who did not were likely to end up in the 15th-century stocks located on the now small village green. St Edward Hall, built in 1878, dominates and its bell-turret accommodates a bell used to summon the fire brigade. The foundations of The Crooked House, built in 1450, rest upon four beehive-shaped bastions. Charles I stayed at the King's Arms Hotel (a coaching inn) in 1645, at the time of the battle of Naseby. The 18th-century Talbot was the town corn exchange. St Edward's Church was built between the 11th and 15th centuries. Its 88ft high bell tower was completed in 1447. Three wool merchants' graves can be seen here – each with a symbolic wool bale on top of its tomb. The Roman Well in Well Lane was the town's water source until mains water was laid in 1937 – it can still pour out 3,000 gallons of water per hour.

Upper Swell

The River Dikler flows through this tiny village which retains the appearance of being from a previous age. By the bridge in Upper Swell there is a fine waterwheel fed by a large pool. The manor house and church are also worth a visit.